R

Foreign Currency Exposure Managem

Foreign Currency Exposure Management

Peter W. Briggs, PhD, MSc, FCA, MCT

Senior Consultant, Touche Ross Management Consultants

London
Butterworths
1987

United Kingdom	Butterworth & Co (Publishers) Ltd, 88 Kingsway, LONDON WC2B 6AB and 61A North Castle Street, EDINBURGH EH2 3LJ
Australia	Butterworths Pty Ltd, SYDNEY, MELBOURNE, BRISBANE, ADELAIDE, PERTH, CANBERRA and HOBART
Canada	Butterworths. A division of Reed Inc., TORONTO and VANCOUVER.
New Zealand	Butterworths of New Zealand Ltd, WELLINGTON and AUCKLAND
Singapore	Butterworth & Co (Asia) Pte Ltd, SINGAPORE
South Africa	Butterworth Publishers (Pty) Ltd, DURBAN and PRETORIA
USA	Butterworths Legal Publishers, ST PAUL, Minnesota, SEATTLE, Washington, BOSTON, Massachusetts, AUSTIN, Texas and D & S Publishers, CLEARWATER, Florida

The views expressed in this book are those of the author, not necessarily those of his employer.

British Library Cataloguing in Publication Data

Briggs, Peter W.
   Foreign currency exposure management.
   1. Foreign exchange administration   2. Risk Management
   I. Title
   658.1'55   HG3851
ISBN 0-406-57090-6

Typeset by Latimer Trend & Company Ltd, Plymouth
Printed and bound in Great Britain by
Billing & Sons Ltd, Worcester

PREFACE

This book is intended to cater for the needs of treasurers, accountants, bankers, finance management and all those other individuals who require to know much, or little, about the control of profits and losses arising from foreign currency holdings.

The financial press is full of comment on company annual reports bemoaning the size of currency losses. It is quite possible that there are equal exchange profits amongst quoted companies, but these profits are often concealed with trading items to deflect the glory onto management. Even so, there are many companies that are not in control of their results as far as foreign currency exposure is concerned. If a technical work can have a mission, the mission of this book is to help the management of these companies who have not yet mastered control of foreign currency exposure. The book may be of use to the professional treasurer to confirm his views, or to supply a slightly different approach to certain problems. The professional user may find this book of most use for reference, whilst the lay reader would need to read it right through and then use it for reference and as an action blueprint.

In order to allow the various methods of use, the book's contents are ordered in a continuing argument in small subdivisions. The first part of each subdivision is a summary of the contents of hat subdivision. Therefore it is possible to skim through the summaries and absorb the main points. Busy managers can seldom spare the time to wade through copious detail. If an important point is still not clear to them, they can spend longer on the section detail.

As a further method of conveying complex points, examples are given in the text and there is a full-scale case study. The case study seeks to bring out as many of the points in the book as possible without creating too complex an example.

The detailed contents of the book cover computation of currency exposure, policy formulation and execution, and the full range of accompanying concerns and services. The chapter on financial instruments includes the latest slick products of the banking community and the chapter on services describes the up to date technology available.

The subject of foreign currency exposure management is complex and unclear to many. In this book the main areas are set out and, I hope, explained in a clear way. The subject is too important to be misunderstood for much longer.

PWB
April 1987

CONTENTS

HISTORY

SUMMARY

For those that consider that the past holds the key to the future, there follows a detailed analysis of the relative values of different currencies from the beginnings of the use of coinage. It is difficult to obtain foreign currency exchange rates for, say, the Middle Ages, but it is possible to find the changes in the purchasing value of particular currencies. If it can be safely assumed that purchasing power was the main determinant of exchange rates until the quite recent increase in the complexity of the foreign exchange (FX) market, then the following analysis is a useful discussion in relation to foreign currency rates from the very earliest times.

For those that consider that the past is a weak determinant of the future of the FX market, go on to the next chapter.

In the beginning

Barter and the currency of goods gave way to coins beginning in 1,000 BC in India, although some form of money was in use in biblical times around 2,000 BC. By the eighth century BC coins were in use in part of Turkey and by the fifth century BC the Greeks were using them. From the outset local shortages or political and social revolutions would vary the value of money. Even in the time of Alexander the Great, one major famine led to charges of speculation by a number of traders, including a certain Cleomenes of Naucratis. Public scepticism of currency dealers has a long history. Coinage had, however, become an important symbol of political unity and was used as such by Alexander to reinforce his empire.

The early Greek or Roman currencies tended to dominate the limited amount of world trade which was carried out with currencies. Therefore interchangeability values of currencies tended to be less important, since most transactions would be in the same currency. With the later waning of the universal empires, importance of local coinages, and hence their interchange values, became more material. For historical analysis it is easiest to assess the purchasing power changes of local currencies and from this to deduce the exchange values of the currencies. Until modern time it is arguable that changes in value of particular currencies was the dominant determinant in their exchange value.

Currency fluctuations were common in the Roman Empire and a foreign exchange market was well established. The biblical money changers were supplying Roman currency to the Jews so that they could pay their taxes to the Roman civil authorities. There is no evidence that Jesus disapproved of the process of money changing even though he did not like the money changers

1

using the Holy Temple as the site of their transactions. FX dealing is still a problem on the Sabbath. The Tokyo Saturday morning market is the only real option.

Social revolution in the third century AD had decimated industry and commerce. Currency depreciation and loss of business initiative and drive had halted external trade. Few coins of the third century have been found in India and external trade was not resumed until order and stability were re-established in the Empire in the Byzantine period. The Byzantine Empire had a period of stability from the seventh century AD to the twelfth century. Western Europe was less stable with the silver denarius of Emperor Charlemagne being quickly debased.

One success story was the English silver penny, or sterling, which became an international currency in the revival of trade of the eleventh and twelfth centuries. This may have been due to the East Anglian wool exports to the Continental weavers which made East Anglia so prosperous and was certainly due to the fact that the coinage was not debased over time. Here was an early example of currency strength generated by a strong trading position coupled with good currency management.

In France there was civil unrest in 1306 when there was a 39% devaluation. Venice had enormous inflation and currency debasement between 1343 and 1354, whilst England had two periods of intense inflation before and after these dates.

In the sixteenth century prices rose five-fold in England and Spain, but less fast in the rest of Europe. The English inflation was blamed at the time on cost of military campaigns, excessive exports, activities of monopolies (the multinationals of former times?) and the speculations of middlemen. Spain's large acquisitions of gold and silver from America was long considered the reason for the inflation, but in fact the traded value of these metals was not depressed at the time and moved independently of the value of money. Currencies had taken on a value not directly related to the metal value of the coinage. There had to be some connection, however, because if the metal in the coins became more valuable than the purchasing power of the coins, those coins would be quickly melted down. This would be why debasement of a coinage was quickly followed by inflation.

The seventeenth century currency fluctuations were more marked in Spain than in the rest of Europe. There were numerous Spanish royal decrees to change the value of the coinage, such as a 50% devaluation in 1628.

The eighteenth century saw two hyperinflations, both linked with political turmoil. The USA from the War of Independence (by 1777 in Virginia a pair of shoes cost $5,000) and France after the Revolution (a debt of 10,000 francs in 1790 had a real value of 35 francs in 1796). In Germany, currency depreciated 35% between 1792 and 1801, with a 21% drop in Spain between 1789 and 1800.

In the nineteenth century in England, currency values fell between 1820 and 1851, with some reversal upwards until 1870, when there was a continued decline until 1896. By this date price levels were 20% below the 1851 level. From 1896 prices rose until after the First World War. Prices on the Continent of Europe showed a generally similar pattern except in Spain where there was a more dramatic early price fall (by 1830 prices were 30% of their 1812 level). Japan opened contacts with the outside world in the nineteenth century. It had initial price falls, no doubt due to wider markets being available, but prices doubled between 1890 and 1914. In the USA the Civil War period produced price rises greater than rest of the world, as would be expected with wartime supply difficulties, but from 1897 to 1914 inflation was still 40%, against, say, 26% in Britain.

It was at this time that the FX market gained significance in London. This arose from the many trade links forged through London with its many commodity exchanges. The merchant banks of London were the main dealers.

During the First World War price rises on the Continent of Europe tended to be larger than those in England and there were wide variations between nations. In Germany and Spain prices doubled; in The Netherlands they rose 2.5 times; in Norway and Sweden they trebled; in France, Belgium and Italy they quadrupled; Finnish prices rose five-fold; Czechoslovak sixteen-fold; and Bulgarian even more. In the US prices doubled whilst Japanese prices rose 1.5 times.

After the First World War the trend of currencies moving in the same direction continued, but this time downwards. In Britain the Cunliffe Committee had concluded that sterling should return to the gold standard at pre-war parities. To achieve this, wholesale prices halved between 1920 and 1922. In France prices fell by one-third, with a 40% drop in Norway and The Netherlands and in Sweden and the USA prices halved. The two exceptions to the normal trend were Italy, with a steeper fall of 75% in prices, and Germany with the ultimate exception of the Weimar Republic hyperinflation. Hyperinflation did also occur in Austria, Hungary, Poland and Russia, but not on the grand scale of Germany (on 15 November 1923 1 US dollar equalled 4,200 billion German Marks).

By the late 1920s the downward trend in prices was widespread in the Western World (with the exception of Spain and Greece with their stable prices). This continued until 1934, when concerted governmental moves to end the Great Depression started to stimulate economic activity again in a trend that continued through the Second World War. There were localised exceptions to this trend, such as a US recession in 1937 which only moderated after monetary expansion measures the following year.

By this time there was certainly better governmental control of exchange rates. Relative inflation rates was not now the dominant determinant of exchange rates although there will always be some connection. After the 1929 US stock market crash, countries became protectionist, imposing tariffs, quotas and exchange controls. This curtailed and distorted trade which often degraded to a bilaterial basis. No one country would reflate and ease trade restrictions, as it was thought that this would cause that country to be flooded with imports whilst there was no large available market for its exports.

In the post-Second World War period world economic conditions and exchange rates were largely determined by US monetary policy. The Bretton Woods system of fixed exchange parities put a damper on exchange movements but could not resist fundamental changes dictated by economic conditions, even though the timing of changes was usually politically inspired. The US dollar became a stabilising influence until large US balance of trade deficits produced an oversupply of dollars and the collapse of the Bretton Woods system. The oil shock of the early 1970s broke the trend of expansion from the previous 20 years. The disappointment of expectations was spreading strains in communities where continuous improvement had come to be taken for granted (Ashworth, 1975). The present foreign exchange (FX) market can be traced back to 1973 when the majority of the world currencies moved to floating exchange rates after the collapse of the Smithsonian Agreement, which had replaced the Bretton Woods system. Prior to this, currency volatility was only a problem when there was an imminent devaluation or revaluation, and it was possible to delay management foreign exchange policy action until those times. The framework had been set up in the early 1950s, after a fragmented pre-war market of many small brokers and some unsavoury practices. With floating exchange rates a total and regular review of the results of volatility became necessary for the first time. Inability to defend fixed parities through the first oil crisis of the early 1970s had forced governments largely to leave their currencies to the mercy of market forces. The so called 'Dirty Floating' of government intervention in the FX market has not been effective. Intervention requires governments to use their gold and currency reserves. Fixed exchange rates were a problem in that governments were forced to intervene to defend the fixed parity. Reserves were either drained or rose excessively, causing inflationary pressures in the domestic economy (exported goods left the country and money in payment returned). In any case, intervention has always tended to be counterproductive, especially if it is obvious to the market. Very few governments have the reserve strength to fight the exchange market and win, although multigovernment rescue packages have succeeded in obtaining the market's respect. For 40 years the International Monetary Fund has been a source of funds to bolster a country's reserves, but recent problems for the IMF in obtaining increases in its quotas from member countries and its reputation for making harsh demands as a condition of making loans, have reduced the popularity of this reserve source. The IMF has an official commitment to a regime of stable but adjustable parities, with provision for floating in particular situations. The present Governor of the Bank of England has professed that the IMF is the international institution which controls currency volatility (Lee Pemberton, 1984) and that the Fund's surveillance should extend to all Fund members, not just borrowers from the fund.

It can be seen from this currency history that currency volatility is not a new phenomenon, although in the past it was normally concurrent with a war or other political turmoil. Volatility of exchange rates in a world of relative political and economic calm does not have so many parallels in history and therefore I do not feel we can draw much from history to deal with the present situation.

BACKGROUND: PRESENT MARKETS

SUMMARY

FX exposure management must take place in the present FX market. This chapter describes the present market and attempts to isolate the broad influences upon it. These influences are certain but their relative effect is ever changing. Perhaps the major prize in the FX market goes to those that can correctly gauge the current mix of influences.

Do not skip this chapter unless you consider yourself already well versed.

The stage for our drama

The formal FX market exists for most convertible currencies and is broadly supported by the international banking community. Governments are large users of the market but are not normally market makers (traders at the core of a market who either buy or sell on demand). Some multinationals and large corporations such as ICI and British Petroleum are taking a market-maker role and in fact BP has formed a separate banking arm which is registered with the Bank of England as a Licensed Deposit Taker. A high degree of competition ensures a near perfect market, trading round the world 24 hours a day. Multinationals should welcome the trend to world coverage markets as it will inevitably lead to a greater range of opportunities at lower costs for the multinationals (Fernie, 1985).

The level of market efficiency is customarily graded by three degrees (Fama, 1979). First there is Weakly Efficient, which implies that past exchange movements cannot be used to forecast future movements. Second there is Semistrong, which denotes that a large and competitive group of market participants have access to the publicly known data significant to future currency movements. Third Strongly Efficient, which requires that the large group of participants has access to all data significant to currency movements. Prominent studies of market efficiency include a number from the US (Poole, 1967, Dooley and Shafer, 1976, Giddy and Duffey, 1975, Logue and Sweeny, 1977, Cornell and Dietrich, 1978, Roll and Solnick, 1975, Kohlhagen, 1975, Rogalski and Vinso, 1977) and one from the UK (Murfin and Ormerod, 1983). The lack of empirical testing of an exhaustive and uniform data base precludes reaching clear-cut conclusions for or against the Efficiency hypothesis (Jaque, 1981). However, from the author's observations (without conclusive theoretical proof) the FX market would fit somewhere between Semistrong and Strong. There is a large body of publicly traded information available to all (sometimes at a price) and also some principal traders are party to other relevant but secret information. Whether these two elements of information comprise all significant data would be very difficult to prove. As a further technical observation, perfectly working speculative markets should not remove all price instability. This is because it is a necessary condition for efficient resource allocation, that in any activity marginal cost equals marginal benefit. Marginal benefit from price stability is a decreasing function of stability and reaches zero when fluctuations are zero. Since the marginal cost of keeping liquid currency funds to stabilise price is always positive, the optimum position must be reached before the point of price stability (Grubel, 1977).

Currency parities have largely been left to market forces as the strongest price determinant. They may be the strongest influence but that does not mean they are particularly rational (for the contrary argument see Levich, 1980). Short-term capital movements can greatly outweigh the volume of settlements for goods and services. Such capital movements can often be influenced by fickle sentiment (Henney, 1985).

A trivial rumour can spark off frenzied movements whilst at other times major changes have no discernable affect. For extended periods since 1979 the US dollar exchange rate, and therefore much of the foreign exchange market, has been strongly influenced by the weekly announcement of the M1 narrow measure of US domestic money supply. The 'market' forms a consensus opinion of what the announcement will be and cautiously moves in response. If the consensus view is proved wrong by the subsequent announcement, this can produce overreacting volatility unwarranted by the actual figure announced. Though the Monetarist School lays great store by money supply figures, the author considers that even they would think the FX market reaction to the M1 announcement excessive. The Stock Market is often criticised as a volatile market, but at least it does not assess the share prices of a company on the basis of the amount of cash and bank current account balances it holds weekly.

The price of oil is another key factor closely watched by the foreign exchange market. Countries with an excess of oil reserves over normal consumption are said to have Petrocurrencies, and are doomed to have their currency rate buffetted by every change in the perceived fortunes of the oil market. Announcements by OPEC can have a greater effect on the FX market than the oil market. That OPEC has difficulty in influencing the oil market is only slowly dawning on FX dealers. When it does, oil will hopefully fall back to its correct weight in the scheme of currency influences. Oil development can pull in foreign capital and strengthen a currency, but the effect is more due to the capital inflow rather than the oil sales. The market anticipation of the oil sales have a greater effect than the oil sales themselves.

The two basic mechanisms of the FX market are 'Foreign Exchange or FX' itself, that is converting one currency to another immediately (called 'spot') or at a predetermined date ('forward'), and 'deposit', which is lending or borrowing in a specified currency. In addition to these basic elements, other products such as currency swaps, futures and options are available to cater for particular needs. Market makers are constantly producing new products but most are variations and combinations of foreign exchange and deposit deals. Many convertible bonds allow a switch in currency and thus can be used to cover exposure. Securities can be broken down into constituent parts. Some parts can be retained, whilst unneeded parts are sold. This stripping of a product to produce various different attributes will almost certainly increase in importance as dealers in the finanical markets become ever more sophisticated.

International trading in a particular currency is normally centred on the principal financial centre in the domestic economy of that currency. Sterling deals flow through London, Deutsche Marks through Frankfurt and US dollars through New York. The funds are held in a local bank account in that financial centre but the person who owns title to those funds may be resident anywhere in the world.

The practical repercussions of this is that participants cannot deal in currency for delivery on a day which is a bank holiday in the principal financial centre of that currency. There is a further complication, in that deals are more difficult to arrange for delivery on a New York bank holiday, as most FX deals are transacted as composite deals through the US dollar. A deal through a German bank to buy French francs for Dutch guilders would normally be covered by the bank in the market as one deal to buy French francs to sell US dollars, and one deal to buy US dollars to sell Dutch guilders.

It would, however, be possible to find a direct market buying French francs for Dutch guilders and this would be organised by French and Dutch banks. These limitations apply to delivery dates only. It is possible to agree a transaction at any time, but as with any market, the best prices are obtained at an hour when the market has the largest number of participants (Briggs, 1984). This normally occurs when the domestic market in that currency is open and no adverse technical factors are at play. Technical factors are influences such as Central Bank rate fixing times, uncertainty before political or financial statements and quarter-end periods when banks often reduce their trading. Special deals for obscure currencies or deals needing to be transacted at less than ideal market hours are probably best done through banks specialising in these currencies.

Differences in time zones can make it difficult for a multinational to achieve instantaneous cash and FX management policies on a truly global basis. However, this is mainly a problem of internal management, not a limitation of the market. The major dealing centres link in a 24-hour cycle (Tokyo, Hong Kong, Singapore, Bahrain, Frankfurt, London, New York and San Francisco).

These are some of the peculiarities of the FX market. There is no overall authority for supervision or as a lender of last resort. The principal Central Banks of the world have long discussed the need for controls on the Euromarket which provides the bulk of the FX market. However, the authorities have not been able to come up with a scheme of effective control that would not seriously hamper the operations of the market. Exchange controls are a method of interference and, where they exist, they are a formidable obstacle to multinational management (Prasad, 1976). Such controls, used by less developed countries, can overvalue their currencies (Crawford, 1985). Devices such as licensing, multiple exchange rates and import deposits are used (Daniels, Ogram and Radebaugh, 1979). A world of 24-hour markets that dwarf central bank reserves, cannot easily be controlled by those central banks (Lipsey, 1985, Fildes, 1985), except when they act in concert, as in the case of the Group of Five countries (USA, Japan, West Germany, France and Britain). Even this effective grouping is hampered by disagreements on who should do what (Harris, 1987). This is caused by the different conditions in each of the countries and resulting policy conflictions. It is much easier to complain that other members are not doing the right thing quickly enough, rather than do something painful yourself. Central bank reserves have doubled in the last ten years but the FX market has increased some eight times in that period (Dale, 1985). The volume of FX trading on the New York market is twice the Gross National Product of the USA (Colchester, 1985) and 15 times trade transaction volume (Spencer, 1984). Market confidence seldom responds to the 'touches of the tiller' and 'deft steering' that the economic fine-tuners would like to administer (Jay, 1985). Even when half-a-dozen central banks enter the market, big dealers do not diverge from any firm trends (Fleet, 1985). The Swiss National Bank has abandoned controlling exchange rates through interventions, as it believes they do not work (Urry, 1984), despite the great importance to Switzerland of export competitiveness (Wicks, 1984). The right solution for central banks is to develop official techniques that vitiate the adverse side effects of an otherwise useful market (Shaw, 1981). Up to the present time there has been a very high standard of conduct in the FX market. As the market broadens with time it is hoped that this high standard will continue, though many suspect that this will not be the case.

The universal acceptance of a very precise code of conduct in the FX market requires that management of a business wishing to trade in the market must have a good knowledge of its workings in order to obtain the best prices. FX dealers bargain long and hard, but will never cheat their customer. Dealing only with the company's clearing banker would be easier but is unlikely to be cheaper.

CURRENCY FORECASTING

SUMMARY

A reliable forecast of what will happen in the FX market is much in demand. It is a pity that such a thing does not really exist at present. The available forecasts have very specific limitations which have to be understood if such forecasts are to be used effectively. The following chapter describes how various interested parties see these limitations. In the end each person forms his own detailed opinion of the usefulness of forecasts (in general and in particular). What is clear is that no one forecast is universally successful, or even approaches that state. Most management decisions require some kind of forecast input. Each manager has to decide on the source and reliability of the forecast he uses. This is arguably the most difficult part of FX management, so do not blame me for not supplying easy answers.

Forecasting services

There are numerous enterprises which offer to prophesy the future movements of exchange rates. This great number is indicative of the profitability of such services. However, the lack of supremacy achieved by any one service also indicates a lack of consistent accuracy. In the best capitalist traditions, such services will be available so long as there are people willing to pay for them.

This is not to say that forecasting services do not have their uses. Every foreign currency management decision requires some element of forecast and this has to be obtained somewhere. A manager either produces his own forecast or he must look to an external source. Even for people principally engaged in foreign currency management it can be difficult to find the time to construct an adequate forecast.

Anyone who uses a bank for their FX dealings, has the opportunity to obtain free advice from the bank dealer. The value of this advice will depend on the quality of the relationship and the level of expertise of the bank. It is as well to cultivate a number of these relationships in order to obtain a range of views and to exclude the particular bias of any one dealer. Dealers have a tendency to 'talk to their book' (eg suggest you buy a currency they have an abundant supply of). This is not necessarily deceitful, as you might expect the dealer to hold a supply of a currency that he believes will increase in value. If he wants to dispose of a currency it will always be quicker (if not cheaper and less obvious) to sell it on the interbank market. Another dealer bias is the very short-term nature of their view. Dealers work in a market changing by the second. They make their profits by switching positions on these very short-term horizons. They have little opportunity to view things from the longer term. Even the forward contract dealer is moving his position on a minute by minute basis and will consider matters on this basis. Any enterprise will have some medium- or long-term factors in its currency considerations. It has, therefore, to have some input other than the bank dealer perspective.

Many practitioners are forced to use professional outside forecasts as they know that their own opinion is not fully researched. Such a decision is not an easy option, as the resulting review and selection process can be almost as bad as constructing your own FX forecast. I am sure that many despair of the review and revert to their own forecast.

For those that persevere with the review, there are three basic types of forecasting service.

1 Economic or fundamental

This is based on the underlying economic factors of countries in relation to each other. Cause and effect relationships are researched between the currency and external factors mainly economic. The type of economic factors are:

(a) government economic policy
   - monetary
   - fiscal;

(b) economic fundamentals
   - balance of trade
   - inflation differentials;

(c) rational market forces; and

(d) technical effects
   - currency blocks
   - effective exchange rates.

Factors are compared to see which currency is in a weak position regarding economic factors and will therefore fall in value on the exchanges. A number of years ago, the measure of inflation used to be critical. The index of export prices was often the best inflation measure but, for instance, for Japan, the wholesale price index was the most useful. Recently interest rate differentials have had far less impact on exchange rates than many economists believe, however, with some notable exceptions such as the US dollar-sterling rate. Many contend that over the short term, interest rate differentials still have a marked immediate effect on exchange rates; on the other hand, Porter (1971) and Dufey and Giddy (1978) argue that economic fundamentals will most certainly establish the trends and turning points over the longer term. Economic models can be put into two categories: extrinsic and intrinsic (Dufey and Mirus, 1982). Extrinsic models work from the basis that key factors have fundamental causal factors that can be fed into the model. Intrinsic models use past values of key factors to forecast their future value. With economic models, there is the basic problem that what is a good model now may quickly become outmoded.

The forecasting methodologies used are multiple regression, discriminant analysis and advanced economic modelling (eg dynamic models). There is the constant problem of assessing whether sufficient economic data has been used and how unquantifiable sentiment factors should be represented. There is also the problem of obtaining precise and timely figures.

Key factors in the economic argument are the theory of purchasing power parity and the equilibrium real rate of exchange. Both are based on the view that there is an exchange rate which balances the economic forces at any one time. Market forces will pull the market rate from this equilibrium price, but the long-term average rate will be this equilibrium price. Of course, even if the long-term average were always this equilibrium price, each actual price could be some distance from the average. Knowing the average price may be of little practical use when it is the actual price which affects you. Such average prices are of most use when an enterprise has complex exposures rather than one currency pair. The larger the number of actual prices the closer the sum of them approximates to the average.

Why is there an equilibrium price? The supporters of the theory argue that if a currency becomes too strong, producers based in that currency will become uncompetitive and will sell less abroad. Imports into that currency area will expand as they become cheaper in that currency terms.

This adverse move in the trade balance of the currency will cause an outflow of funds and a consequent loss in confidence by holders of the currency. This loss of confidence will tend to depress the exchange rate back towards the equilibrium price. Even the supporters concede that the corrections will not be exact, and therefore the exchange rate will tend to overshoot downwards and trigger a reverse reaction as the currency becomes too competitive. The main point is that these movements will be around the equilibrium price.

The above argument appears to be very neat and believable. Unfortunately, lag factors and market inconsistences make what actually happens quite different, at least in the short term. In the short term, economic forecasts have recently been singularly unimpressive. Such forecasts take into account rational market movements as part of the equation. Unfortunately, short-term currency market movements exhibit a significant level of irrationality. All the more annoying for the economic theorists has been the fact that a much less elegant method of forecasting has taken the short-term forecasting prize. This method is technical analysis.

2 Technical or chartist

The adherents to this method contend that market movements work in patterns which are forecastable. Chartists look for emerging patterns on graphs tracking currency movements. Similar methods are used for many different prices, not just FX rates. Prices are plotted on the graphs in different ways.

There is the straightforward continuous curve of, say, closing prices, which is easy to construct. As a refinement of this, for each day's plot a bar is shown linking the highest and lowest price traded that day with possibly a side dash to mark the closing price (see the bar chart in Fig 1 below). Such a bar chart shows volatility and is easy to compare with other time series.

The variations do not stop there, a point and figure chart plots the direction of price changes. Rising prices are plotted as, say, an 'x' in a vertical column. If prices start to fall the plot is moved one place to the right, and, say, an 'o' is plotted downwards. The 'o' column continues until prices rise again when there is another move to the right to start an 'x' column. You will note that for this chart there is no regular time axis to the chart because the progression across the chart depends on changes in price direction, not elapsed time. For an example of a point and figure chart see Fig 2 below. The point and figure chart highlights significant moves.

The chartists have not stopped at straight price plotting in their quest for the meaningful measure. They plot the rate of price change in strength and direction. Oscillators and momentum charts of various types are used to try to highlight trends. Different forecasters prefer different methods, but there is merit in using various methods in order to look for similar trends occurring when the charts are compared: the so-called rule of multiple techniques.

The method of plotting long- and short-term moving averages on the same graph can show important inter-relationships. The points where the moving averages cross are considered significant by some technical analysts.

In all the different methods, the chartists hope to spot standard shapes (such as that resembling a head and shoulders in a simple price plot graph) very early in their formation. Once the familiar shape is spotted, the chartists consider that they can prophesy future trends until the familiar pattern subsides. Patterns of support and resistance are important movements to isolate. A resistence level is a price which is judged by all buyers in a market to be the highest sustainable. As the price reaches that level some holders will sell to take a profit because there is a general feeling that prices will rise no further. This selling may yield sufficient currency to satisfy any purchasers. Therefore the price rises to the resistance level perhaps a number of times, but does not breach it. Chartists consider it very important if the resistance level is exceeded by other than a small over-correction. Such a breach can indicate a new, higher, general market view of a maximum price for the currency. In such situations significant price rises can occur.

A support level is the exact reverse of a resistance level. It is a level which appears to be the minimum the market considers appropriate for a currency. Again a significant breach of this level is thought to indicate a consistent and possible dramatic drop in price.

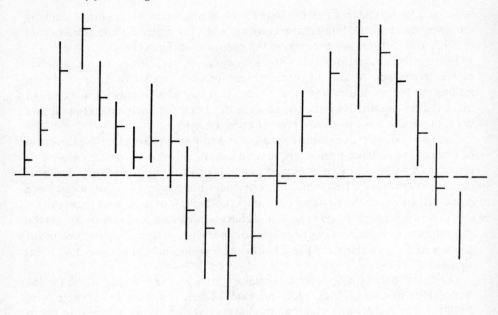

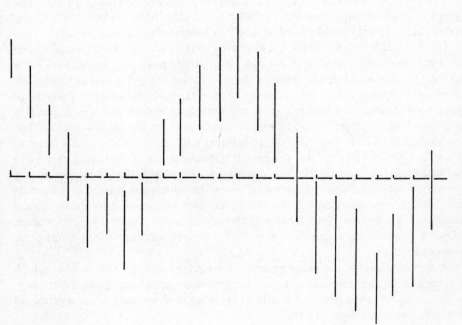

Fig 1

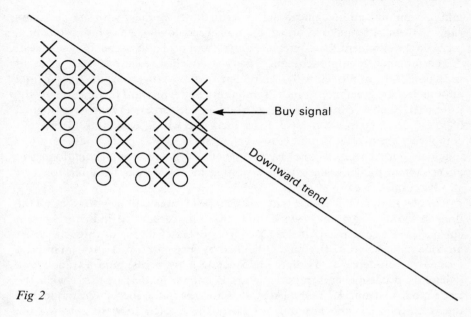

Fig 2

Trends in rises and falls in price can also be studied. In Fig 2 above, a downward trend resistance level is plotted. A consistent move across this trend line is thought to show a reappraisal by the market and a possible sharp reverse in prices. Therefore, in Fig 2, the move across the trend line is marked as a buy signal for investors looking for an increase in prices.

Calculative techniques are also finding their way into chartism. A relative strength index is calculated using a number of days' higher and lower closing prices. The index figures are supposed to show trend reversals before they become apparent from the chart. Certain theoretical methods are also popular with chartists. Ralph Elliot, a nineteenth century economist, described a natural rhythm in his book modestly entitled *Nature's Law—the Secret of the Universe*. Chartists look for these natural rhythms to show trends.

Technical models work with manifest trends whether those trends are rational or irrational. It is a behavioural science. Supporters contend that the going price in the market reflects all the available information on supply and demand. The price movements reflect the market's psychology. A more cynical view is that if enough people follow the technical models, the results become self-fulfilling prophecies.

3 Judgmental

This describes a less formal approach with an expert in a particular currency taking economic and technical factors and tempering these with market views ranging from rumours to informed opinion. Techniques such as brain storming, scenario development, cross-impact analysis and probability encoding are used.

The judgmental approach can be very useful in predicting when an event prophesied by a model will occur. The major danger in the judgmental approach is the great importance of weighting of the relevant factors used by the forecaster. Such weighting is highly subjective. The forecaster may have isolated all the correct factors but have given them the wrong weighting to produce completely the wrong result. However, as Wyss (1982) points out, very few judgmental forecasters will not have some underlying idea of an equation, as in an economic model. The existence of this model should be some form of steadying influence.

Ross Jackson (1983) asserts that no one type of model is likely to work all the time, although each may work quite well in certain periods for certain currencies. He contends that the FX market operates in one of three modes at any one time. A speculative mode (dictated by speculative pressure), an interest mode (where interest rate differentials dictate movements), and a trade mode (where the prime mover is trade demand). Economic models are useful when the trade mode is strongest. Technical models are best in the speculative mode. For the interest mode one has only to study the quoted forward rate for the currencies, as this is directly related to interest differentials. An extension of the trade mode might be termed the market mode. This recognises that most of the volume in the FX market is now capital flow related, rather than trade flow related. Many of these capital flows are generated by banks. Bank dealings make up some 90% of the London FX market.

If the FX market were a perfect one, the whole market would have all forecast information, and taking the advice of a forecaster would not benefit a dealer in the market. As the market is not perfect, a composition of various forecasts should help a dealer. Even so, in a 1978 survey of corporate treasurers, 58.4% of respondents felt that currency forecasting was the weakest link in their risk management programme (Evans, Folks and Jilling, 1978). There is no reason to hope that this scepticism has since mellowed as FX markets have become more volatile in recent years.

Euromoney publication conducts a regular survey of the success of currency forecasts. There has been no continually best survey, but use of two surveys with action when they agree, is definitely superior to using any one survey. However using three surveys tends to confuse matters (Jaycobs, 1984, Ramond, 1984, Bilson, 1984). The important thing is to spot the right signal on which to act.

The lack of success of forecasts is not necessarily due to the poor quality of forecasters. Lord Keynes, one of the most eminent economists, was very successful at speculating in the commodity markets. However, his most disastrous ventures, from which he had to be rescued by his father in the 1920s, were in the FX market of which he was a lifelong student.

For those who want to try their hand at technical analysis, there are micro-based computer programs which will do much of the trending work for you. For the major currencies, there are Prestel-based systems to allow you to input exchange rate information automatically. You have the information in the form the professionals use, but you have to remember that interpretation is not the easiest part of technical analysis.

In spite of all the short-comings, a corporate treasurer is likely to obtain a better indication of a currency's future value from a carefully prepared forecast, than from a naive extrapolation of past trends: not that such extrapolations are totally without use.

Mathematical models

A major problem with any mathematical model that will adequately forecast exchange rate movements, is the need for a large and changing number of input parameters. The factors that dictate exchange rate fluctuations are arguably so numerous and changeable, that all attempts to limit input sources to manageable proportions has seriously stunted the usefulness of those models. This can be seen from the lack of any consistently performing model available to the business market. The problems governments have with FX also indicates that the public sector does not have effective models.

The author does not consider that there is a general lack of the expertise necessary to construct an effective model, just that the parameters are very complex, and redundancy within any model may occur at erratic intervals. Though these suggestions may seem radical to some, they are shared by many practical people within the FX market.

An illustration of the complexity of FX market models is clear from the necessary equation to calculate the amount received at maturity for a 90-day debt receivable in a currency and financed in that currency, but to be remitted to a parent company in another currency (Babbel, 1982).

Two factors in the equation are cursorily described as random variables. These are the future spot rate at the nineteenth day and the standard deviation of this factor. What has to be said, is that both these factors are not known with certainty until after the equation has lost its usefulness. Therefore, even with this forecast with the most modest of scopes, a complex parameter has to be included. Basic uncertainty modelling may be of some use (Fama and Miller, 1972) and the advent of cheap computer power at least now makes this type of forecast feasible in cost effective terms. How soon this feasibility will extend to general purpose exchange forecasts is less clear. Truly chaotic phenomena can never be accounted for, but according to emerging theory, simple mathematics can now start to predict what happens when order breaks down. This could give the necessary structure for forecasts, but will not necessarily limit the parameters.

Mathematical equations and models have a much greater use in calculating the sensitivity of a business to any currency changes that occur, rather than trying to estimate the currency changes. In the parallel area of interest rate sensitivity, gap and duration models are gaining acceptability and widespread use.

CURRENCY CHARACTERISTICS

SUMMARY

This chapter starts with a broad description of the currency blocks and their relationships. Volatility in currency values arising from the floating of exchange rates is then examined. Finally the argument proceeds to a detailed review of characteristics from the perspective of how those characteristics affect world trade and multinational companies. If the detail starts to wear you down, skip to the next chapter: financial instruments are much more interesting.

Distinctive currencies

The important world currencies are forming into distinctive blocks. These are groups of currencies which move in value in broad sympathy with each other. Many of these sympathetic movements exist because the authorities responsible for managing those currencies are deliberately tying their currency to another currency in the group. Other currencies are tied to another for technical trade reasons such as oil producers dependence on the US dollar.

These main blocks which are emerging are the US dollar, the European Monetary System and the Japanese yen. Many other currencies exhibit tracking tendencies for one and sometimes two of these blocks.

In addition to these blocks are the compound currencies. These are baskets of currencies put together by supranational organisations. The two main ones are the IMF's Special Drawing Rights and the EEC's European Currency Unit. The amounts of constituent currencies that make up each unit are held stable for long periods. Therefore the value of each unit fluctuates in response to the price movements of the underlying currencies.

Volatility stemming from floating

The transition to floating exchange rates by most of the principal world currencies by 1973, had important implications for macro-economic policy. The roles for monetary and fiscal policy were in effect reversed (Robinson, 1983). By refraining from intervening in exchange markets, central banks could control domestic money supply and, in principle, influence domestic economic activity and price level. Fiscal policy, on the other hand, without a complementary monetary policy, would now be relatively ineffective for influencing domestic economic activity, since changes in the same direction would simply bring about alterations in the interest rate and the exchange rate, offsetting the primary influence of the fiscal change. It took a while for governments to realise that the change of emphasis was necessary, but it was as much the transition to floating, as the blandishments of Milton Friedman and the Chicago School, that caused governments to become monetarist.

UK policy-makers had been convinced of the virtues of fixed exchange rates in the 1950s and 1960s and although they were forced into floating sterling in early 1973 as a result of a serious currency crisis rather than by choice, they soon accepted the new conditions with enthusiasm, but with a less than full understanding, and with disastrous results. Floating the exchange rate (which some academics and financial journalists had long been urging on the government) seemed to provide escape from balance of payments constraints which, so it was thought, were the principal cause of the UK's poor real economic performance. In practice, however, the elasticity of demand for imports and exports is seldom equal and there are lags in the automatic supply and demand balance (Carter and Partington, 1981). With slow appreciation of the implications of a floating exchange rate on domestic monetary policy, in the 12 months following the float in June 1972 money supply increased by 30% and by another 20% over the following year. With these excessive increases, the pound/US dollar exchange rate fell from $2.60 in June 1972 to $2.38 in mid-1974, a fall which continued through 1975 as money supply continued a fast rise. It is not surprising that UK retail prices rose by 70% during the three years following floating (although part of this was due to the world rise in oil and other commodity prices at this time).

From the UK example it can be seen that governments took some time to get used to and to master the new conditions (Whittam Smith, 1984). Badly-phrased UK government announcements have had a turbulent affect on sterling (Jones and Lipsey, 1985). As a basic tenet, public discussion of a currency crisis tends to worsen it (Galbraith, 1974). The continued apparent random and volatile movements of currencies either indicates that their understanding and control is still less than perfect or, more likely, exact control is too painful in domestic policy terms.

The European Monetary System currencies have remained well ordered against each other, without painful government action. There has been a convergence of financial policy by members (Dennis and Nellis, 1984). The EMS has been a good advertisement for currency areas (Bailey, 1985) (Moreland, 1985).

The strong US dollar in the first half of the 1980s is perhaps an example of external exchange rate and internal policy conflictions. US exporters had bemoaned the 'over-valued' dollar, but the US administration had not taken the most strident steps possible to correct the situation. Perhaps they considered the cost too high in disrupting steady growth in the domestic economy. Brittan (1985) considers that such internal policies have a crucial effect on the US dollar.

Surprisingly the statistics on exporting goods from the USA in this strong dollar period belied the exporter's concern. Exports from the USA in 1982 to

1984 were increasing despite the strengthening dollar (Beresford and Pearson, 1985), not that the strong dollar did not greatly stimulate imports into the USA to produce the large external trade deficit (Hosenball and Whymant, 1985). It is probably the quick changes in currency value which are most disruptive to trade (Smith, 1985).

Certainly the large US budget deficit has sucked in overseas funds and kept the US dollar buoyant at least until the mid-1980s (Blundell-Wignall and Chouraqui, 1984, Hogg, 1985). 1985 was the year in which the US, the richest and most powerful nation on earth, became a debtor to the international community (Kaletsky, 1985). However, the deficit can only be reversed slowly to avoid throwing the world into recession, with the loss of the US market for world exports (Srodes, 1984). The US budget and balance of payments deficits have stayed large since 1985, even though the US dollar has weakened on the foreign exchanges. Japan was a very large US dollar investor by 1985 and the position has since compounded, but will these funds stay in the USA?

Professor Alan Budd (1985) of the London Business School contends that Thatcherite and Reaganomic policy can cause exchange instability, as they use direct controls. The present buoyancy of FX markets is due to the growth of indebtedness. The traditional exporters of capital, ie OPEC and the USA, have progressively moved into deficit (Develle, 1984) which needs financing, and there are few large sources of such finance.

There have been a number of studies on the causes of over and undershootir.g of currency value movements (Dornbusch, 1976, Bhandari, 1981, Driskill, 1981, Gazioglou, 1982, Gazioglou, 1984, Niehaus, 1977, and Buiter and Miller, 1981). The closest consensus conclusion is that exchange rate overshooting occurs with a sufficiently high degree of capital mobility (provided that a rise in domestic prices raises domestic interest rates), whilst undershooting occurs in conditions of relatively low capital mobility.

Certainly companies involved in international trade and investment tend to the view that exchange uncertainty is their most pervasive risk (Plasschaert, 1979). As a contrary view, a Rockefeller Foundation survey in 1980 to obtain banker's and multinational's experience of floating, found them generally in favour of floating currencies, though it took more management time (Bannock, Baxter and Rees, 1984).

Hogan and Pearce (1984) radically conclude that, nothing is more damaging to international trade than unstable exchange rates. Whatever governments or central banks agree in the near future, multinationals will have to live with exchange rate uncertainty.

Effects on world trade and multinational companies

In early 1983 it was noted by George Schultz (US Secretary of State) that the yen/dollar exchange rate had moved down 20% and then moved back up again by the same amount in the space of a seven-month period the year before. He concluded that the problem warranted close study by the major currency countries (Schultz, 1983). Alexandre Lamfalussy, economic advisor to the Bank of International Settlements further considered that it was hard to imagine that the volatility of such a key price as the exchange rate could have anything other than an adverse influence on economic decision making. It created a climate of uncertainty which was bound to have an adverse impact on decisions concerning investment, production and trade (Lamfalussy, 1983). Akio Morita, chairman of Sony of Japan, put the business view when he said that if the value of a currency fluctuates widely for reasons entirely unrelated to the business involved, then it would not be difficult to understand that normal economic activity suffers as a result (Morita, 1983). The previous Governor of the Bank of England, Lord Richardson, also pointed out that one must suspect that exchange markets have displayed a persistent tendency to overshoot and have produced greater volatility than was justified by underlying conditions (Richardson, 1983).

In the last 15 years there has certainly been a weakening in world trade. The volume of world trade had grown at an average annual rate of 8.5% in the period 1963 to 1972. For the 1972–1979 period the average increase was only 6% and for 1980 and 1981 there was no increase. Although a number of factors would have contributed to this trend, the fact of exchange rate volatility in the same period naturally prompts the questions about the possibility of a causal link.

In any discussion on exchange rate volatility it is easy to be drawn into an argument as to the appropriate level relationship for any two currencies. When an exchange rate movement is only reversed after a considerable time, any apparent misalignment during the ensuing period may well appear to observers as a problem of the exchange rate level (Williamson, 1983). Thus an indisputable distinction between the results of fluctuations in rates of exchange and inappropriate levels is not sustainable.

The exchange rate volatility of the currencies of the major industrial countries is the main area to concentrate on. It is true that the exchange rates of other countries, particularly less developed countries, show considerable volatility, it is the degree of movement among the major currencies that constitutes the exchange rate environment within which other countries must plan their policies. Any particular multinational company may have important connections with a specific developing country which make the volatility of that country's currency material. Generally speaking, however, such currencies are tied or influenced by trading blocks. From 1973, all the currencies of the major industrialised countries were floating. There were the same number of developing countries with floating currencies in 1975 as there were in 1970, however, and even in 1983 still only one in five was a floater. Systems of tying the rates of the developing countries did change in this period. From the original system of linking rates to a single currency such as the dollar, the developing countries have now opted for a basket of currencies. In 1983 some 37 developing countries had opted for a basket, with the dollar and the French franc still popular constituents. In 1970, 26 countries tied their currency to sterling, but by 1983 the Gambia was the only remaining one. The use of baskets is not limited to developing countries; Finland, New Zealand, Norway and Sweden also use them. The move to baskets strengthens the effect of the major currencies which tend to be strongly represented in the baskets. Baskets will also limit volatility to influences on basket constituents.

It is an accepted proposition in economics, that economic agents are risk averse, so that greater risks either get built into prices, or reduce quantities supplied and demanded at a given price. If only the source of uncertainty in international trade related to exchange rate, it would probably be undeniable that greater variability in exchange rates inhibited trade (Clark, 1973, Hooper and Kohlhagen, 1978). There are, however, many forms of uncertainty to which economic agents are exposed and it is not necessarily the case that exchange rate violatility is independent of the others (Friedman, 1953). As a most obvious example, if exchange rates move to offset divergencies in the underlying inflation rates, the uncertainties facing multinationals might be less than in a situation where inflation rates continued to diverge, but exchange rates remained constant (Pigott, Sweeney and Willett, 1975). Similarly, where balance of payments pressures have previously been dealt with by changes in trade restrictions, resort to greater movements may simply substitute price uncertainty for equally important uncertainties about administrative restraints on trade (Johnson, 1969).

Empirical testing of the effect of exchange rate volatility would ideally seek a measure of the net additional uncertainty introduced by exchange rate variability in any period. In the absence of such a measure, the only available approach, and the one adopted by virtually all researchers in the field, is to use observed exchange rate variability as a measure of uncertainty. If no adverse consequences for trading are detected, the conclusion is either that the uncertainty costs are small or that they have been systematically offset by countervailing changes in other elements of uncertainty. There is great difficulty in separating the effects of exchange rate uncertainty from those of other and related economic features.

In addition to increasing costs through uncertainty, exchange rate movements may require costly shifts of a multinational's resources between economic activities in response to changing price incentives (Kreinen and Heller, 1974). As the exchange rate for a given currency moves down, a wider range of products become profitable to produce and export. For currencies that are strengthening, the size of the foreign trade sector tends to shrink correspondingly. Thus multinationals may be induced in favourable currency areas to develop markets and install production capacity that turns out to be unprofitable when exchange rates move against those areas.

The above effect is referred to in the IMF Annual Report for 1982. It states that although little direct evidence is currently available on costs of such swings in resource allocation, it seems likely that they have contributed to uncertainty about the profitability or unprofitability of various industries and may thereby have inhibited fixed capital formation, particularly in countries with a large foreign trade sector. In addition, because goods and labour markets are far from being perfectly efficient, such swings can contribute to wasteful investment and to unemployment.

The kind of exchange rate fluctuations that give rise to adjustments of cost are likely to be those that persist for a protracted period. A multinational's investment and production decisions are rarely changed in response to short-term moves in profitability, nor will such short-term moves affect the viability of the company (Williamson, 1983). The fact that exchange rates have become more volatile may well reduce the responsiveness of resources allocation decisions to relative price changes, at least in the short term (McKinnon, 1978). Businesses may be reluctant to change existing patterns of resource use and trade flows until they are persuaded that a given exchange rate change will not soon be reversed. It is likely that only relatively long lasting departures from the norm will cause decisions to be taken which, in more stable times, would not have been taken.

It is particularly difficult to make a quantitative assessment of cost of exchange movements. They may not show up in a reduction in the volume of trade, since the ebb and flow of trade shares among countries may be offsetting in totality. To the extent that exchange movements do have an effect on trade flows, this may work through to reducing levels of output and investment and to creating higher levels of frictional unemployment. Since such an influence would not necessarily alter the relationship between trade and its other determinants, there would not necessarily be any residual effect to be explained by exchange rate factors.

Perhaps some indication of the degree of influence that is taking place in the external position is provided by developments in the balance of payments current account for the country in question.

As well as influencing patterns of trade, exchange rate volatility can have an impact on the patterns of international investment. A multinational business, in deciding where to situate new investment, has to take into account not only technical factors affecting cost, but also the uncertainties of currency relationships. This may lead to a diversification of investment, even at some cost to efficiency, in order to minimise the risk stemming from currency movements. Instead of concentrating production facilities in the lowest cost location, they may be located in a number of different currency areas. At least the multinational enterprise has the option of spreading its risk in this way. A single currency based enterprise has to suffer all the swings of its currency with little chance of offset.

Where investment diversification has occurred it may appear to be in response to exchange rate uncertainty. However, in the majority of cases it is more likely to be in response to the perceived prospective level of the rate and any uncertainty in this perception. There will also be cases where the determinant is in other economic and political uncertainties that are manifest in the rate of exchange. When a multinational decides to invest abroad to diversify its exchange rate risk, the risk it is likely to be most concerned about is the level around which the exchange rate is likely to fluctuate, rather than the size of month to month or quarter to quarter fluctuations that cancel each other out. Such a company will also be more concerned with exchange rate movements that affect its cost of production, relative to its sales return, rather than just the nominal value of one currency in terms of another. A company could prefer to invest in a country that has a well established exchange rate mechanism to ensure that domestic costs and prices do not get too far out of an appropriate international alignment, rather than in a currency area where nominal exchange rate volatility is less, but exchange rate 'stickiness' resulted in more uncertainty about real rates and hence profitability.

As exchange rate volatility will affect the price of those goods traded internationally it may well become more attractive to produce goods and services that are not traded internationally. Goods and services traded only domestically are often of lower technology than those traded internationally so that this also would give a reduction in investment.

A volatile exchange rate will favour the most efficient producer, as he will have a greater profit cushion to weather currency downturns in advantage. Within limits, this is good as the mechanism by which economic resources are redirected over time to the most appropriate business. Such monopolistic tendencies are bad for the economy as a whole and could harm the company by removing the stimulus to innovation and productivity. Countries would tend to specialise and as they became the sole producers could become insulated from the type of economic forces which should be influencing the companies.

Exchange rate turbulence has relatively greater adverse consequences for developing than for developed countries (Helleiner, 1981). Although most multinationls are based in developed countries, they often trade with less developed countries and there is a new breed of multinational rising fast, which has its base in developing countries. These are groups such as Birla of India, United Laboratories from the Philippines and Autlan in Mexico.

For developing countries, since trade is less frequently denominated in the domestic currency, traders face a greater measure of uncertainty, especially because forward exchange rate markets are less readily available or more expensive. When a developing country pegs its currency to that of a major trading partner and therefore floats against the currencies of other industrialised countries, this creates a preference for bilateral trade with the country to which it is pegged. There was presumably a strong trading relationship in the first case in order to justify the link. Such a tendency foregoes the benefits of multilateral trading relationships and causes a less than full exploitation of comparative advantage. A further potential disadvantage arises from the premium which variable exchange rates place on responsiveness and flexibility in production and trade.

The fundamental uncertainty in business is that unforeseen movements in revenue relative to cost can make a particular transaction or activity uneconomic. When revenue and cost is in different currencies, clearly an important dimension of this uncertainty is the possibility of exchange rate moves. They may not be an independent source of uncertainty, nor do they affect different multinationals in the same way.

The simplest kind of international transaction is of the type where a trader contracts to buy a fixed quantity of goods at a given price in a foreign country. His profit is the difference between the purchase price and the selling price, less freight, insurance and interest costs, and the only source of uncertainty is the exchange rate by which he can translate his sales revenue in foreign currency into local currency to repay his borrowing. The exchange uncertainty is the possible movement in the spot rate over the period of the contract. For currencies where a forward market exists, it is possible for the trader to remove this uncertainty by taking out a forward contract for his trading contract period. The forward price may be more favourable than the current spot price, so that he earns more apparent profit on the deal; the real profit or loss on a forward contract is the forward price matched against the spot price at the maturity of the contract. Charges (called the 'spread') by banks for arranging short-term forwards rarely exceed 0.2% and quotes can easily be obtained for terms of up to one year. Longer periods have greater spreads but these are still not excessive. A currency option can often be used as an alternative hedge instrument, although it will cost more than a forward contract.

Most international trade, however, has a longer time horizon than the simple transaction described above. There is the commitment of resources and development of markets over an extended period of time. Over this time all the factors of production can be affected by currency movements in addition to the effect on sales. The commitment period for resources can vary considerably. The decision to market excess production can be affected at short notice, then not repeated if market conditions change. In a different product considerable modification may be necessary before it can be sold to any one foreign country. Here excess capacity cannot be switched around to the country with the most favourable exchange rate. In the third case where local production is required, there is virtually no possibility of short-term switching.

From the foregoing, it is clear that different kinds of uncertainty are important to different multinationals. There is no unique measure of 'exchange rate variability' that can be used as a proxy for the uncertainty and resultant cost which businesses face as a result of exchange rate moves (Lanyi and Suss, 1982). Four dimensions of variability of relevance to multinationals are:

1 nominal or real exchange rates;

2 bilateral or effective rates;

3 time span of variability; and

4 predicted versus actual exchange rate movements.

In considering whether nominal or real rates are the most relevant, time scale is important. In the very short term inflation differentials are insignificant, except where hyperinflations are involved, so that nominal rates are the most relevant. As the time scale increases, inflation differentials increase. With the purchasing power parity theory of exchange rate movements, in the long run inflation differentials are the only significant determinant of exchange rates. Over very long time periods, this appears to be true. The choice is, then, which price index to use as the measure of inflation differentials for real rates. Reference to an inappropriate price index can systematically affect judgments on the scope and direction of movements in real exchange rates (Williamson, 1983). It is generally argued (Artus, 1978) that the index used should attempt to measure cost of production of traded goods rather than the actual price of those goods. This is because the forces of competition will tend to equalise the finished goods' prices by pressuring profit margins. This view has led to the favouring of indexes of unit labour cost in manufacturing industry, but this ignores extractive and agricultural costs. Therefore the wider gross domestic product deflator is the best measure.

In regard to bilateral versus effective or multinational exchange rates, each separate international transaction takes place between two currencies and therefore involves only one bilateral exchange rate. From this it might seem that the appropriate measure of uncertainty is some average of relevant bilateral rates (Lanyi and Suss, 1982). This reasoning overlooks the actual and potential diversification that characterises international trading relationships. If currency A has a systematic tendency to rise against currency B when currency C falls, the average or effective exchange rate for B may be much more stable than either of the two bilateral rates. For a multinational with various currencies the effective exchange rate best reflects the aggregate uncertainty in their income stream. Bilateral exchange rates would be the appropriate concern for simple single currency trading as in the case where imports are dominated by a single major supplier.

In relation to the time span of variability, volatility will alter. The average of opening and closing rates will vary depending on whether day-to-day, quarter-to-quarter, or year-to-year swings are considered. As exchange rates show serial correlation (that is, the level of the rate in any period is strongly connected to its level in the preceding period), it is important to assess how much the exchange rate has moved since the preceding period and how far it has moved relative to some average or trend. As exchange rates vary continuously, it might seem appropriate to measure volatility over very short periods. Trade transactions take place at individual moments and the possibility of continual rate movements imposes uncertainties on companies, even if these are quickly reversed. It is not, however, these short-term movements that are the main cause of disquiet.

Companies tend to look at each transaction, so that the time scale of the money flows of each transaction is important. If a company produces goods in one month and is paid for their sale three months after, it is quarterly exchange movements that most interest the company. For a company setting up an operation abroad the transaction period is much longer than for individual supply contracts.

Inter-period movements that reverse themselves will not be considered important by the company. What is important is any sustained deviation from the trend, as well as period to period movements. If exchange rates move by an average of say, 2% a month in a random manner, this may well be an easier type of uncertainty for a company to absorb than where monthly movements are only 1%, but tend to accumulate in the same direction before reversal.

As multinationals use different planning horizons, depending on the nature of the activity in which they are engaged, there is no single correct time period for gauging exchange rate volatility.

For predicted versus actual movements in exchange rates, in so far as actual rates have been well predicted in the past, companies will be less concerned with uncertainty. Therefore the use of actual to predicted deviations in exchange rates will be some measure of exchange rate uncertainty.

In applying statistical techniques to exchange variability, it is worth noting some of the difficulties in generating statistical estimates of variability. Standard deviation is traditionally particularly useful for analysis. It has been pointed out (Westerfield, 1977), however, that these properties depend on assumptions about the underlying statistical series that are not borne out in the case of exchange rates. The skewdness of the distribution, particularly in the fixed rate period when the bulk of the observed variance is accounted for by individual discrete exchange rate changes, means that observed standard deviations do not necessarily have the normal properties. Average changes would appear to be a better measure.

There is no doubt that, on most definitions of exchange rate volatility, fluctuations in exchange rates have been greater in the decade since floating exchange rates were adopted than they were in the period of fixed exchange rates in the 1960s. The weighted average of the monthly changes in nominal effective exchange rates among the major industrialised countries was 0.2% during the period 1961–70 and has averaged almost 1.2% over the period 1974–82, a sixfold increase. Quarterly movements in nominal exchange rates, which are somewhat larger than average monthly movements, have also increased around six times. When real exchange rates are considered, volatility is found to have been greater in the 1960s than for nominal rates and for the late 1970s real rates were less variable. None the less, the weighted average of changes in real rates has still been three times greater in the period 1974–82 than in the 1960s. Indeed for no year after 1974 is the average variability of the seven major currencies (Canada, France, Germany, Italy, Japan, UK and USA) less than for the year of greater variability in the 1960s.

Has there been a learning process during the floating rate period, such that volatility has tended to diminish as experience with floating rates accumulates? For most measures of monthly, or quarterly, variations in exchange rates, 1973 is the year of greatest volatility. However, although there was an apparently systematic trend towards greater stability over the following five years, this trend has been interrupted at the end of the 1970s. Japan and the USA have shown greater nominal and real fluctuations since 1978, whilst Italy and the UK have the greater fluctuations in the mid-1970s. Therefore, there is no clear evidence of a trend towards greater or less volatility over time.

Different currencies experience differing volatility at different times. This might indicate a country-inspired connection with exchange volatility. Certainly some currencies tend to be more stable than others over time. The real exchange rates of France, West Germany, Italy and Canada have shown considerably smaller quarter-to-quarter movements in the eight years from 1974 compared with the US, UK and Japan. The EMS and its predecessors may account for the stability in the first three European currencies.

There is general acceptance of the purchasing power parity theory that prolonged inflation differentials among countries will eventually lead to broadly offsetting exchange movements. The reason for the relationship is well explored (Officer, 1976), and has been borne out by the movement of some currencies. High inflation in Italy, UK and France have depreciated more over time than low inflation Japan.

A study of deviations from any general trend in the period 1961 to 1982 for Canada, Japan, USA, Italy, West Germany, France and UK show a deviation of only 2 to 3%. There is also no evidence of an increasing trend of volatility about longer term trends, with the USA showing increased volatility from the mid-1970s whilst the EMS shows a consistent level of volatility.

A simple test of the effect of exchange rate volatility on world trade is to trace what has happened to the growth in world trade. An investigation (Blackhurst and Tumlir, 1978) of the extent to which the increase in world trade exceeded the increase in world output for the period from 1958 to 1978 was extended by the IMF up to 1982. The investigation did not show any special characteristics for the period of floating currencies when more currency rate volatility has occurred. A further study (Bergsten and Cline, 1982), indicates that international trade flows tend to be more responsive to cyclical factors as trade grows faster than output during cyclical upswings. From these two studies there seems to be no evidence that any special feature in the recent past, such as exchange rate volatility, has had an independent negative effect on the level of trade. It can always be argued that such surveys have a limited time span on which to make universal judgments and also that the cyclical effects may themselves be due partly to exchange volatility. Despite these limitations, it does represent a useful result.

There are early studies which focus on the last century and the inter-war years (Yeager, 1976). These found little evidence of an adverse impact of exchange rate volatility on trade. For a review of an early floating exchange rate period, there is research on the Canadian dollar in the period 1952–70 (Clark and Haulk, 1972) which included the period up to 1962 when the Canadian dollar floated. This study concluded that there was greater exchange rate volatility during the float period but nominal exchange rate volatility did not adversely affect Canadian trade. A further study up to 1973 which included West Germany, Japan, UK and Canada again detected no systematic relationship between volatility and trade.

Yet another study (Hooper and Kohlagen, 1978), takes the period to 1975 and breaks trade flows down to their constituent bilateral movements. They reported

'We found absolutely no significant effect of exchange risk on the volume of trade (at the 0.95 [confidence] level), despite considerable effort and experimentation with alternative risk proxies and functional forms of the quantity equation.'

An investigation of Brazil for the period 1957-75 shows periods of relative stability and extreme volatility in the cruzeiro/dollar exchange rate. Export volumes in 22 sectors of manufacturing and primary products were significantly impacted by the periods of extreme volatility, but although the evidence is suggestive, even the authors of the survey suggested caution. Other changes in the Brazilian economy occurred at the same time as the volatility and periods of economic growth accompanied the period of stability. These factors are also likely to have affected the export trade.

A survey of real exchange rate variability (Cushman, 1983), took 14 sets of bilateral trade flows and showed that eight were not affected by rate volatility and six were. As the Brazil survey (mentioned previously) and the Cushman study were both using real exchange rate volatility, there does seem to be some small effect of real exchange rate volatility on trade flows.

Studies of the exchange volatility effect on trade growth showed no effect (Kenen, 1979), and in two surveys by the same author (Abrams, 1980) one showed an effect and an amending one showed no effect.

Cross-section analysis attempting to show whether a change in the export/ GNP ratio in the 1973–77 period varied between countries depending on variability in their exchange rates, used both nominal and real exchange rates and wholesale and consumer prices, but still found no significant correlation between exchange and export/GNP change (Thursby, 1981). Thursby undertook further analysis based on bilateral export flows with three statistical measures of exchange volatility (nominal and two price adjusted rates) for 20 countries. Volatility had no significant affect in 90% of cases. Therefore there is some evidence that exchange volatility uncertainty inhibits trade. The fact that the bilateral tests solely show the effect may be due to the overwhelming influence of other factors in aggregate trade flows.

A poll of participants in international trade is another method of obtaining an impression of the effect of exchange rate volatility on world trade. The Federal Reserve Bank of Boston undertook such a poll following the float of the Canadian dollar in 1970. The 156 participating US companies with trade in Canadian dollars all reported no influence on their trade flows due to Canadian dollar volatility. It should be noted, however, that the Canadian dollar was relatively stable against the US dollar over the period of the survey.

A later study (Duerr, 1977) did not pose specific questions on the effect of exchange volatility and trade, but from a panel of 75 representatives of major US manufacturing firms the great majority agreed that floating had made the practice of international business much more difficult. At least some of the panelists were more concerned with substantial trends and swings in exchange rates rather than short-term volatility.

A survey in 1981 (Blin, Greenbaum and Jacobs, 1981) polled 27 companies in Canada, USA and UK to preview exchange hedging prevalence. It found that firms had adapted to the reality of volatile exchange and did 'not appear to have refrained from increasing their foreign investment in the face of rate uncertainties'. This finding would, presumably, have been the same for volatility effects on trade.

Bearing directly on the effect of exchange rate volatility and trade is a survey by the Group of Thirty (1980). Banks and major international corporations in five countries were polled. All said that floating had had a negligible impact on the level of foreign trade and foreign investment and costs and prices.

Exchange rate volatility can potentially lead to shifts in the allocation of resources as producers' international competitiveness varies. Even where the competitiveness variation is temporary, there can be adjustment costs such as short-term unemployment, retraining and adaption of plant (Kreinen and Heller, 1974). However, some producers may view the exchange rate movements as temporary and only react to moves that they consider long term (McKinnon, 1978).

There is an argument that small enterprises suffer more from exchange rate volatility than larger enterprises (Helleiner, 1981). Certainly there is a certain minimum amount of management time required to monitor exchange movement whatever the size of the organisation. This minimum will represent a greater proportion of total management resources for a small business. Also smaller organisations are normally less diverse and therefore have less likelihood of producing natural netting of foreign currency exposures. The larger an organisation is, the more likely that if one division has an asset in one currency, another division may have a counterbalancing liability in the same currency.

Input price uncertainty is considered to be one of the motives behind vertical integration (McCulloch, 1983). As exchange rate volatility is a factor in price uncertainty, such volatility can be said to be a motive behind vertical integration in a market. There is, however, no evidence that it is a decisive factor or even a material factor in many cases.

There is one argument that postulates that exchange rate volatility may actually increase international trade. If a country is a marginal producer of a product, exchange volatility may be the final disadvantage that ends production. The country would henceforth have to import that product, thus increasing international trade.

It is alleged that investment decisions are negatively impacted by exchange rate volatility (Hieronymi, 1983). If volatility increases business uncertainty, it might dissuade some investors in long-term projects. However, surveys such as the Group of Thirty (1980) show no such reluctance by the larger organisations and Kenen (1979) detects nothing in the overall foreign investment figures for 1973–76.

From the previously stated extensive analysis, it is clear that there is little in the way of directly measureable adverse effects on trade of exchange rate volatility. As uncertainty is considered bad for economic activity this may seem surprising. The findings may suffer from the inadequacy of the statistical methods used. Possibly such lags occur in the economy, that the empirical tests were misread. However, in view of the wide range of surveys and the differing populations used, fundamental errors seem unlikely. What probably is true, is that there is great difficulty in separating the independent effect of exchange rate volatility from the impact of other changes in the economic environment (Williamson, 1983). McCulloch (1983) considers that, of the large number of commercial activity risks, exchange rate volatility may be a relatively minor one. The other surveys would not seem to discredit this view.

It must be remembered that an exchange rate is a price and that price is set to balance supply and demand. As part of this supply and demand represents payment for traded goods, it could be argued that it is the trade which is affecting the volatility, not vice-versa. The very volatility may be short-term balancing of trade supply/demand disequilibrium.

It would seem better to smooth exchange rate 'overshooting' volatility, which produces temporary false price signals to distort the allocation of resources. It is, however, difficult to determine whether a given exchange rate move represents an erratic swing or a shift to a new equilibrium position. Exchange rates determine and respond to capital flows as well as trade flows and capital policy imperatives may be different from those for trade. As the accumulation of relatively liquid capital in any one economy is much greater than the value of trade taking place at any one time, it is not surprising that changes in the desire to hold capital in any one currency can have such a marked effect on the exchange rate.

TREASURY INSTRUMENTS

SUMMARY

This chapter describes aspects of the many financial instruments and techniques used in FX management.

The tools of the trade

There are various techniques available to a multinational in its quest to manage foreign currency exposure.

Currency netting systems

Netting is a method, not an instrument, but it is appropriate to include it here as it is important to apply it before hedging and covering by financial instrument is considered. Netting is the process of off-setting like currency assets and liabilities to show the net currency exposure of a business. Care must be taken with net items which are not capable of off-set within a reasonable time-scale. Blocked currency items would come under this heading.

Fig 3 below shows how the payment flows can be simplified. You will note that the diagram assumes that the payments move directly from one subsidiary to another. In fact some at least will flow via various banks, so that a netting can cut out more flows than are shown on the diagram. It is probable that there were many different currencies involved in the payments in the pre-netting situation. When netting has been instituted, it is possible for each subsidiary to make one net settlement, in its own currency, with the netting centre. This should reduce the currency dealing problems of the subsidiary.

There is an argument for netting across groups of currencies which tend to track each other by official agreement or market tendency. Such group netting must, however, be carefully monitored for any break-up in the value tracking of the group. The Dutch guilder was always thought to shadow the Deutsche Mark until an EMS re-alignment, when the Dutch government decided to impose a different change in value from that of the Deutsche Mark. It is interesting to note that the exchange market reacted angrily to this and put the guilder under considerable speculative pressure, which automatically pushed the guilder even further from the Mark. Commentators noted at the time that the Dutch government had learnt its lesson. This lesson is presumably that no government has absolute control over an international currency, even with a minor trading currency such as the guilder. The multinational concern has considerable scope for netting by re-assessing the currencies of investments,

Fig 3
Before—Payments by one group subsidiary to another

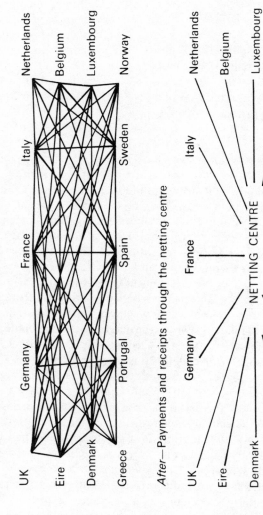

After—Payments and receipts through the netting centre

divestitures and trade flows. Netting is often based in US dollars as a convenient benchmark and the European Currency Unit is gaining popularity for netting. If a significant element of non-European currencies needs to be covered the SDR, the Special Drawing Right unit of the International Monetary Fund, may be more appropriate.

Netting is normally achieved by the use of a computer database management system on any size of machine from a mainframe to a micro. The major international banks often offer their own system to encourage customers to use the bank's dealing room for FX deals. The system is often very attractively priced to encourage purchase. The bank can make much more from the FX dealing than it could from putting a premium price on the system and making fewer sales.

The different systems operate in a similar way, except in the method of isolating cashflows. Systems either work on the payment inputs (that is the person making a payment initiates an entry) or payment and receipt input (both payers and payees enter amounts). With both receipts and payments into the system, there has to be a reconciliation stage to remove inconsistencies, such as an expected receipt not being input by the payer. There have to be strict rules set up to settle these disagreements. Many users of such netting systems regard these rigid disciplines as an important added advantage of a netting system.

A standard sequence for a netting system would be as follows:

DAY 1 – NOTIFICATION DAY. Members of the netting inform the netting centre of their amounts. The netting centre calculates a matrix of receipts and payments to each member using current indication FX rates. Each member is then sent details of all his receipts and payments in case he wishes to revise them; he might find he is receiving more cash than he expected and can afford to settle more of his own debts.

DAY 2. Update the matrix with final returns from the subsidiaries. FX deals can now be transacted using figures extracted from the matrix. When the FX dealing is complete, a final update of the matrix is made using actual dealing figures. The subsidiaries can now be sent firm details of receipts and payments to be made in two days' time.

DAY 4. Settlements made

Some netting will not use all these steps, but the general trend of processing is common.

It is important to note that the FX deals transacted on the basis of the initial netting run will not be exactly those required. This is because the initial relationship was built on the basis of indication FX rates. The actual dealing rates obtained will be different from the indication rates. It is important to tell the FX dealer, before dealing, that the quoted amounts are estimates which will vary slightly. If you explain that you are dealing for a netting system, he will understand. If you have used recent indication rates, the final currency amounts should not be very different from the initial amounts. After you have produced your final printout, you should inform the FX dealers that you dealt with what the final amounts are. This should be done as a matter of courtesy; the differences are unlikely materially to move the dealer's currency position and it would be sufficient to notify his backoffice for payment purposes.

Considerable savings in FX costs can be achieved with a netting system. The largest savings are obtained when receipts and payments of each currency are similar in value and the total value of transactions is large. It is often worthwhile building the volume through a netting system even though there are few initial complementary currency flows. It is arranging the volume of transactions which takes the time. You want to be in a position to benefit from complementary currency flows later. An efficient system should not cost that much to run, whilst good matches are awaited.

The European operation of a US multinational with 15 European subsidiaries and sales of US$ 300 m per annum, estimated that it saved US$ 600,000 each year from using a netting system. This was:

- US$ 250 thousand from saved dealing commissions and bought/sold spreads;

- US$ 250 thousand from improved FX dealing rates:

- US$ 100 thousand from the elimination of one day's transfer float.

Re-invoicing centres

A reinvoicing centre is a netting system which includes outside parties. It therefore has the advantages of extending the netting process, but requires that dealings with the outside parties be carefully organised. It is much more difficult to persuade customers, rather than fellow group companies, to pay on a specific day.

Forward exchange contracts

One of the oldest instruments of exposure management and still one of the most popular. In 1979, 85% of multinationals were using forwards (Channon and Jalland, 1979) and they are still the more favoured method of FX exposure cover for corporate treasuries. As there are so many participants in the market, prices for the major currencies for standard periods (eg one month not 27 days or 35 days) are quite keen. A price (not necessarily a very good one) can be obtained for most currencies for any period, up to five years, 24 hours a day. As trading occurs in Europe, the USA and the Far East, there is always one market open for business at any time. Many international banks and companies maintain a presence in these markets in order to be able to adjust their exposure at any time. Their constant dealing makes for an orderly market. The forward price, either a premium or discount, is always closely tied to the difference in interest rates in the two currencies. If the deal is transacted with other than a substantial bank, the element of fulfilment risk, the risk that the counter-party will not meet his obligation at maturity, must be considered.

There are two types of maturity setting for forward contracts. A fixed date contract matures on a set date agreed when the contract is made. An option date contract has a range of maturity dates agreed when the contract is taken out. An option date forward contract is not to be confused with a currency option, which will be described later in this chapter. With an option date contract, the purchaser has the option to call for execution of the forward at any time within the range of maturity dates. It is possible to obtain a contract with a very large range of possible maturity dates, but it must be remembered that the rate set for the contract is the worst rate that occurs in the option period. The FX dealer has to cover the possibility that maturity will be required on this worst date. As it is normal that selection of the demanded maturity date has no connection with the price of forward deals, rather it has to do with when funds are received, the option contract will be an expensive form of cover.

Range forwards

Another variation on the forward contract is the range forward. This is similar to a standard forward contract but there is a range of maturity prices. This range is set partly by the purchaser of the instrument and partly by the seller. The purchaser decides on a minimum price that he requires to be covered. The seller then determines how much upside potential he is willing to allow the purchaser and sets an upper price at that maximum. Then at maturity, reference is made to the then spot exchange rate of the two currencies which are the subject of the range forward. If the spot price is within the specified range agreed for the range forward, the actual spot is used. If the spot is below the minimum, the minimum is used and if the spot is above the maximum the maximum is used. Range forwards are available against the US dollar for sterling, yen, French franc, Swiss franc, Deutsche Mark, Canadian dollar and the ECU.

One advantage of the range forward is that it allows some chance to profit from currency movements in the contract purchaser's favour but does not require him to make an initial premium payment. The high premium costs of near the money options, has dissuaded many treasurers from using currency options. While they are ready in principle to use options, non-returnable premiums of, say, 5% of the principal sum work out to be very large payments to make, with very little immediate apparent benefit.

The disadvantage of range forwards is that the exchange profit potential is small compared with many options due to a small agreed range. It must be said though that it is up to the purchaser how large the range is. If he is willing to set the downside risk at an extreme point, then the upside rate can be higher. There is a further disadvantage that range forwards have to be delivered at maturity, whereas an option does not have to be exercised.

Take the example of a US importer of Swiss goods, who is concerned that the Swiss franc will appreciate soon. A forward contract would be at a rate of 1.60 rather than the present spot rate of 1.68. Such a low rate would dent the profits so the importer might consider a range forward with a minimum price at a small but adequate profit on sales. He would then share in any upside in the US$/SFR rate that might occur.

Deposit and borrow

This achieves the same effect as a forward contract but is undertaken in the cash market (actual principal sums are used). When a customer transacts a swap with a bank, that bank will often create the deal 'through the swap', that is, it will borrow the funds to be received in the future and deposit the funds to be paid away in the future. The customer could have done this himself, but it would probably cost him more than the forward (his borrowing rate will be high and his deposit rate low) and it would add to the size of his balance sheet unnecessarily. A customer may use the deposit and borrow alternative if he is uncertain when the payments and receipts at maturity will actually take place. He can do overnight deposits and borrowings until the funds are needed. This should be cheaper than an option forward contract.

Export tender risk avoidance (EXTRA)

This contract is designed to help sterling based exporters submitting tenders to US-dollar-based purchasers. The EXTRA entitles the seller to compensation if the US dollar falls against sterling should the tender be accepted. Cover is up to a maximum of $2.5 m, with a fee which varies with the principal amount. The bank agrees to repay to the seller a proportion of the fee should the tender be unsuccessful.

Futures contracts

A newer instrument than the forward contract, there are various types of futures contract. In relation to currencies, there are interest rate futures and exchange rate futures. The interest rate futures are not designed as a currency fluctuation management tool, rather they seek to control interest rate costs. It is the exchange rate futures that are relevant to currency management, although they represent less than 20% by value of financial future trading.

Examples of exchanges and their products, available at the time of writing, are given below:

Chicago Board of Trade (from the MidAmerica Exchange) – sterling, Swiss francs, Deutsche Marks and yen.

Chicago Mercantile Exchange – sterling, Swiss francs, Deutsche Marks, yen, Canadian dollars, ECU, Australian dollars and French francs.

London LIFFE – sterling, Swiss francs, Deutsche Marks and yen.

New York Finex – the ECU.

New Zealand Futures Exchange – NZ dollars.

Singapore SIMEX – Deutsche Marks, sterling and yen.

Sydney Futures Exchange – Australian dollars.

Toronto Futures Exchange – Canadian dollars.

All these futures are based on exchange rates to the US dollar.

A number of these exchanges are linked together so that contracts bought on one exchange can be sold on another. The Singapore SIMEX is linked with the Chicago Mercantile Exchange. It is also to be hoped that this linking of trading will encourage trading in the Far Eastern markets, which can be very thin at times. Some US traders are wary of putting trades through SIMEX because it can be difficult to liquidate contracts in the thin market there. There can also be technical problems if the Chicago market has gone limit up (reached the top of the permitted trading range) at its close. The Singapore market would therefore not have a starting price and effectively cannot trade that future until Chicago re-opens the next day.

Another approach to continuous trading in currency futures has been taken by the Chicago Board of Trade. It has applied for the US government regulatory body, the Commodity Futures Commission, for permission to extend trading hours to up to 24 hours a day.

In order to deal on an exchange you have to complete a form of customer agreement with an exchange member. This is a comprehensive description of the duties and responsibilities of the member and the acceptance of trading rules and risks by the customer. Procedures for handling initial and variation margin also have to be agreed.

The margin is the collateral to guarantee performance of the currency contract. The clearing house for the exchange is the guarantor of every transaction carried out on the exchange. It is only willing to offer this guarantee because it obtains deposits from both buyers and sellers. The amount of the deposit, or margin, is set to cover adverse price movements of the futures contract. The first assessment of the necessary deposit is called the initial margin and is paid to the clearing house when the deal is first agreed. A typical initial margin would be from 0.2% to 3%. Price fluctuations each day will vary the price of the future. The whole of the price fluctuation as at close on the previous business day is exactly reflected in what is called the variation margin, which is added or subtracted from the current margin balance each day. If the current margin balance falls below the level of the initial margin, this difference has to be made good by the customer. Profits on futures which push the margin balance above the initial margin level can be repaid to the customer. Only the initial margin level has to be maintained.

The clearing house of the exchange normally funds its operating costs from interest received on investing the margin amounts. Members are required to take margins from their customers at least of a similar amount to that required by the exchange. If the member takes a customer margin greater than that he has to lodge with the exchange, he can benefit from investing the excess. Otherwise the member obtains a return by charging a dealing commission to the customer. The commission is for both buying and selling a future (a round trip) and is payable when the future is closed out or delivery takes place.

If a contract is held until delivery, settlement takes place through the clearing house with the customer having to pay the full cost of the contract, less the margin balance, against delivery of the currency specified in the contract. Very few futures contracts are allowed to remain outstanding until delivery.

Futures allow a customer to hedge or speculate in a currency without investing more than a margin, rather than the full capital value at risk. For the speculator this gives higher potential return for a given investment than a cash market speculation.

The customer will sell a future if he thinks a currency will decline in value, and buy a future if he thinks the currency will rise in value. It might seem odd that you can sell a future before you buy it, but remember the clearing house merely stands between buyers and sellers. For all the futures held there must be another party oversold in the instrument. The oversold position is easily settled by buying an identical contract in the market; the oversold customer does not have to find the customer who bought the original future he sold and buy it back. In fact the oversold customer would have no way of tracing the original future as the clearing house will not tell you who the other party to a trade is.

Interest in futures is currently fading. The two large Chicago exchanges, which account for some 75% of all futures trading, are turning their attention to options. The view is widely held that 95% of possible innovation in futures has already been achieved. Perhaps the future of the future is just as an element in options on futures contracts: the expansion in the Chicago market of this type of option has been dramatic.

In assessing whether a future is good value it is necessary to cost the alternative methods of producing the same cover.

1 A cash market forward contract.
2 A spot rate contract and a currency deposit or loan until maturity.
3 A spot rate contract and interest rate futures to the maturity date.

These are arbitrage possibilities as each produces the same cover. As you would expect, most arbitrage opportunities are closed out by professional dealers before very long.

Unless futures happen to be cheaper than forwards, they do not have any distinct advantages over forwards and are in many ways more complicated. Daily margin payments have to be settled for a future, which is not necessary for a forward. It is possible that a company in a very weak financial decision might find it difficult to obtain an FX forward dealing facility with a bank but could obtain a futures dealing arrangement (as the bank's customer risk on the future is covered by the margin deposit from the customer). However, I do not think that this situation would occur often in practice. FX business is too profitable for banks to refuse dealing lines in all but the very worst cases.

Currency options

One of the newest tools of exposure management (they have been actively traded in London only since 1983), options are fast gaining acceptance by multinationals. As with most options, the purchaser buys the right, but not the obligation, to buy or sell a currency at a pre-arranged price. A call option relates to selling a currency, whilst a put option gives the right to buy a currency. Currency options are traded on exchanges (originally Philadelphia and Amsterdam but now in most centres) and by certain large banks (the over-the-counter market). Examples of international exchanges and the currency options available at the time of writing, are:

Chicago Board Option Exchange – yen, Canadian dollar, Deutsche Mark, French franc, sterling, Australian dollar and Swiss franc;

Chicago Mercantile Exchange – Deutsche Mark, sterling, yen, Canadian dollar and Swiss franc;

European Options Exchange (Amsterdam) – Deutsche Mark, sterling, ECU and guilder;

LIFFE (London) – sterling and Deutsche Mark;

London Stock Exchange – Deutsche Mark and sterling;

Montreal Exchange – Canadian dollar;

Philadelphia Stock Exchange – yen, Canadian dollar, Deutsche Mark, French franc, sterling, ECU, Australian dollar and Swiss franc;

Sydney – Australian dollar;

Vancouver Stock Exchange – Canadian dollar.

Exchange quoted options are usually based on the US dollar; for example, a sterling call option would give the right to buy sterling with US dollars.

There follows the specification of one of the option contracts traded on the Philadelphia Stock Exchange.

Currency – sterling
Currency units – 12,500
Exercise price intervals – 5 US cents
Exercise price and premium quotations – cents/units
Minimum premium change – 0.05
Minimum contract price charge – US$ 6.25
Expiration months – March, June, September and December
Expiration cycles – 3,6,9 and 12 months
Last trading – 1.30pm local time on the last business day before expiration
Expiration date – Saturday preceding the third Wednesday of the month.

Options have taken over from futures as the expanding exchange traded instrument. The bank over-the-counter options are often hedged by the writer bank with exchange traded options. The hedge may be complete or as near as is available on the exchange.

The differences between exchange over-the-counter are as follows:

	Exchange traded	*Over-the-counter*
Contract terms	Standardised	Tailored
Underlying	Physical currency or currency future	Physical currency
Expiration	Standardised	Tailored
Transaction method	Open outcry, auction or market-maker	Direct contact
Secondary market	Continuous	Informal
Commissions	Negotiable (on size)	In premium
Dealers	Exchange members and their clients	Banks and their customers
Pricing	Widely published	Quoted on request

The pricing of options is based on computer modelling of the future value or cost of the instrument. Normally the Black-Scholes pricing model is used. The model is based on a number of assumptions, such as that the exchange rate is a random variable. The Black-Scholes model was constructed to forecast movements in the stock-market and has been amended a number of times to cope with different types of instruments. It is questionable whether it is entirely appropriate to the FX market. Other factors in an option price are as follows.

(i) What is the strike price of the option? This is the price at which the purchaser can opt to deal or exercise the option. Is it at-the-money (the same as the present market price), is it out-of-the-money (below the present market price), or is it in-the-money (above the present market price)? The closer the strike price of an out-of-the-money option to the present market price the more expensive the option.

(ii) Is it an American or European option? An American option can be exercised at any time before maturity. A European option can only be exercised at maturity. An American option is therefore always at least as valuable as a European option and normally more so.

(iii)What does the holder receive if he exercises the option? If he receives immediate cash rather than a future or forward, the option will cost more. This is because the writer of a cash option has to support it with cash to the full value, whilst, say, a future can be supported with just a margin payment of up to 3% of the full value.

(iv)The length of time that the option exists. This is the period that the writer is on risk and therefore the longer the period the more expensive the option.

(v) The interest rate differential between the two currencies. This is quite a minor factor in the option price, which is surprising as it is the overriding determinant of a forward contract price.

The market or at-the-money value of an option depends on whether it is an American or European option. An American call for a currency at a premium (eg Deutsche Marks) is at-the-money when the strike price is equal to the spot rate. However, for a discount currency it is at-the-money when the strike price is equal to the forward rate to maturity. For an American put option at-the-money is the forward rate for premium currencies and at the spot rate for discount currencies. For European options at-the-money is always the forward rate.

A carefully constructed option package can be a very effective hedging instrument. The present high cost of currency options is some deterrent to their use but hopefully, as the market develops the price will drop. There are also ways of buying options that reduce the cost. Option strategies are one way of doing this. A strategy is a sequence of separate options which fit together to produce an overall result. If this sequence includes purchases and sales of options, then the cost will be the net cost of purchases less sales. This may well be less than a simple option purchase to cover a similar risk. The zero-cost option is a strategy of exactly matching option income and expenditure. It is debateable whether exactly covering cost should be a criteria in setting the strike price of an option written. It might be better to decide on the basis of other portfolio criteria and just accept the overall profit or loss.

For the cheapest cost of cover the purchaser has to assess the level of loss on an exchange which would be an unacceptable burden for the business. This would be the strike price for the option to be bought. As the price is set at an extreme level, it should be well out-of-the-money and thus have a low premium. It should then be considered whether some of the potential profit on the exposure could be profitably sold by writing an option. This requires an assessment as to whether the premium that would be received is great enough to recompense for the profit limitation. Many a business would prefer a certain sum rather than a future possible sum. The future profit forecast has also to be discounted at a ruling interest rate because the premium is received now for most options, whilst the profit is in the future.

Even so, the higher the degree of uncertainty about future exchange rates, the greater the risk premium a person will be willing to pay. Options have the advantages of a forward contract and fewer disadvantages. Limitations and rules on exercising options do vary, but the holder has the discretion as regards exercising an option, whereas a forward contract has to be performed at maturity, even if unfavourable to the holder.

If an option is used as a hedge tool, it is unfair to cost it solely as a hedge. The point is, that it also has an appreciation element which is of an investment nature. To say whether an option is more or less expensive than complete forward cover, the investment element of the option has to be split out. There are techniques for splitting the option by constructing a synthetic option with the same result. The pricing and different influences of the constituents can be seen. It is probably not worth going to these ends, but just to remember that the option has more than one benefit element and not to judge it on one alone.

An example of an option in comparison with forwards is shown in the graph in Fig 4 below. The graph shows the profit to a UK company selling in US dollars at differing exchange rates. One line is the profit with a 100% forward cover, another with 20% forward cover and the third depicts the profit possible with a European option with strike price US$ 1.40. The forwards and the option are for the same maturity date. The option is a European option so as to give a better comparison with the forward contracts.

It is clear how different profit potential arises with the different instruments and with different degrees of cover. Deciding the most profitable cause requires some decision as to future FX rates. In the graph example, if the spot rate at maturity is under 1.30 the 100% forward is the most profitable course. If the maturity spot rate is between 1.30 and 1.50 the 20% forward is the most profitable. Finally, if the maturity spot rate is higher than 1.50 the call option

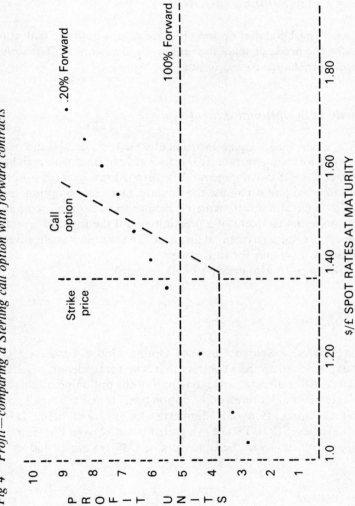

Fig 4   Profit—comparing a Sterling call option with forward contracts

produces the greatest benefit. It can be seen how a forecast of the maturity spot price is necessary to decide which hedging method to use. The forecasts do not have to be very accurate, but they do have to read the correct trend.

Bearer exchange option (BERO)

This is a sterling/US dollar option of a face value of only £5,000. It is designed to cater for the needs of small to medium-sized customers. The terms are very similar to an exchange traded option.

Forwards with optional exit (fox)

The fox is a currency hedging instrument which is a compound of a currency option and a forward contract. It is a forward contract with a right to reverse the contract if it is disadvantageous. The forward rate granted is not as good as a normal forward and if you use the forward cancellation option you normally have to pay a fee at maturity which is similar to an option premium. There is, however, no initial payment of a premium and if the forward is settled there is no apparent premium payment at any time. The premium is effectively collected in the less advantageous forward price.

This instrument is also called a break forward.

Pooled option

Sometimes called a Shared Currency Option Under Tender (SCOUT). The party that intends to award a contract that is up for tender arranges this form of group cover. All tendering parties pay part of the option premium, but only the successful tender bidder receives the option benefits and at a small proportion of the total premium. It avoids duplicate option cover being taken out by tendering parties. SCOUTS are available for terms from one month upwards. All major currencies from the equivalent of US$ 1m are available.

Currency swap

A currency swap is in many ways like a very long-term forward contract. There will often be an initial exchange of currencies, which does not occur with a forward, and a bank is not always the organiser of the transaction, as it is with a forward. The contract is basically an initial exchange of currencies and a future reversing exchange. It is usual for a bank to stand between various parties so

Fig 5

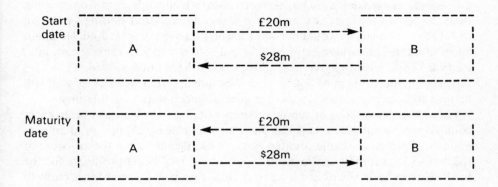

that there is some degree of reciprical movement where the needs of the parties do not exactly match. As principal sums are swapped at the start and maturity, there is no principal sum lent or borrowed, unless you consider it both lent and borrowed. There is no net principal sum outstanding during the term of the swap. The simplest swap is shown in Fig 5 above.

The agreement was that an equal amount of sterling and US dollars would be exchanged at the start and maturity of the swap. The FX rates agreed normally bear some relation to the spot FX rate at the start date. As you would expect, the spot rate at maturity is bound to be different from the rate agreed for the swap. One party will make an exchange profit from the transaction and one will make a loss. In the example above, if the spot rate for sterling against US dollars at the maturity date is 1.30, then party A could have obtained £10m for US$ 26m on the spot market. He has to pay US$ 28m because of his swap contract and therefore he has lost US$ 2m on the transaction. Party B has gained US$ 2m from the deal. It should not be forgotten that both parties have gained the certainty of knowing what their future currency liability in currency was. Possibly A transacted a very profitable piece of US dollar business which he would not have risked without the protection of the swap. He might still emerge with an overall profit which he considers acceptable. Swaps do not necessarily mean that someone has to lose overall, even though someone does usually lose on the swap itself.

As was pointed out above, a bank usually stands between the parties of a swap to lessen the credit risk (this tends to assume that the bank is a better credit risk than the parties, which is not always true). The bank can also function as an active dealer in swaps rather than a passive intermediary. It is possible that no counter-party can be found that exactly matches the needs of a customer wanting to transact a swap.

If there is a general view in the FX market that a currency will weaken, there will be a number of customers wanting to swap to protect against loss from the fall, but not many who want to transact a swap which stops them from gaining from the fall. In the above example, if A was convinced that sterling would fall to 1.30 to the dollar, he would not want to enter into the swap at 1.40. He might agree to a rate somewhere between 1.30 and 1.40 in order to achieve certainty. Party B would have to agree to the lower rate if he wanted a swap.

The swap market is most liquid when there are differing views as to what will happen to currency values, or there is general uncertainty and volatility.

Given that for reasons of supply or simply timing there may not be an exact counter-party available, a bank can serve a useful role in taking a swap onto its books without an available counter-party. It can decide to run the exposure of the swap which it may consider has a good chance of being profitable for the bank. However, as swaps are long term in nature it is unusual for a bank to want to leave them unmatched for their whole term.

There is often a tendency for customers in one time zone all to want to deal one way. Therefore banks that operate in more than one time zone stand a better chance of achieving a match of deals.

The currency swaps market is older than the interest rate swaps market but is much less sophisticated and developed. In 1986, interest rate swaps transacted in London were around US$ 300b in total, whilst currency swaps were some US$ 40b. The market is maturing in the major currencies the US dollar, sterling, yen, Deutsche Mark, Swiss franc, Canadian dollar and ECU. Even so, the risks of holding large swap books is high and large contracts get sold off in transactions involving as many as five counter-parties.

The banks have been ingenious in devising hedges for swaps. They mix and split currency and interest rate swaps and use futures, US Treasuries and sterling gilts positions to create a match. A typical inter-relationship is shown opposite in Fig 6.

The swap dealer must decide which swaps he needs to hold with only short-term cover, because he considers that there will soon be a counter-party available for long-term cover. Some of the large American banks have very large swap books to give customers an instant fit to their requirements. One has a thick computer printout which is revised and handed out to its dealers daily.

In addition to currency mis-matches, there can also be maturity mis-matches which are much more difficult to hedge from the outset. The maturity mis-matches in the swap book of the bank should be aggegated with maturity mis-matches in other instruments and loans, as there might be an offset overall.

For currency swaps between US$ 25m and US$ 250m it is often worth a customer considering a hi-tech swap. This is a specially tailored management package. The idea is to incorporate interesting tax and accounting aspects in the package. Because of the amount of expert time needed to construct the package, it is seldom worth the cost for a swap under US$ 25m. Over US$ 250m one

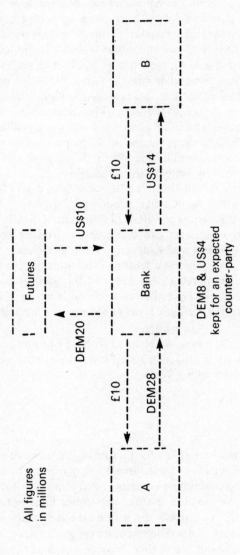

Fig 6

All figures
in millions

market-maker has difficulty in dealing with it, so unwieldy syndicates have to be formed.

Currency swaps have an important role for the large borrowers in creating cheap borrowings. First-quality names can borrow in certain currencies at very low rates. They then swap these borrowings into currencies they actually need and produce cheaper financing than a direct borrowing in the needed currency. It is reckoned that 80% of eurobond issues are immediately swapped. The Australian dollar, New Zealand dollar, ECU and yen have been used in this way. The issues are made when windows arise through a combination of interest rate and currency fluctuations. Borrowers and banks have to move quickly once the window opens, to set up the swap. The cheap rates are often due to the fact that small investors in obscure markets are more willing to invest in a well known international enterprise and will accept a lower return than perhaps a professional investor would. The World Bank is one of the largest currency swappers and certainly benefits from the above effect.

There is also the point that certain borrowing markets have a smaller yield differential between the quality grades of borrower. The Swiss market is supposed to have a narrower differential than the US dollar market. This means that lower-rated borrowers can consistently produce cheaper US dollars by borrowing Swiss francs and swapping into US dollars.

Swap pricing is very much a factor of the price of alternatives in the FX and capital markets, tempered by the needs of the parties to the swap.

The large US banks have the resources to offer large corporations a whole package for issuing a currency bond (underwriting, etc) and the swap to convert it.

The swap market has now extended to offer options on swaps, or swaptions. Like any other option, this instrument gives the purchaser the right, but not the obligation, to undertake a swap.

Factoring

The term factoring here refers to the sale of the debts of a company to another legal entity. The object is to sell currency debts for an immediate local currency amount. Of course, factoring is mainly used as a way of raising finance, but the currency affect can also be useful. This other legal entity could be inside or outside the group. If outside the group, the debts are effectively sold at the current spot FX rate. Sale of debts inside the group does not directly change the group FX exposure, although there may be a partial neutralising effect (such as where US dollar debt is sold to an American fellow subsidiary).

The advantage of intergroup debt sales arises where FX exposures are collected by this means in a finance company where they can be better controlled by specialised management.

The finance company would buy the debts of the subsidiaries on an 'arm's-length' basis. A method often used is to pay the subsidiary at the forward FX rate appropriate for the date when the debt is due for collection. Therefore a debt with three-month credit terms would be purchased at the three-month forward rate. The subsidiary would be in the same position as if it had covered the debt to maturity.

The operations and advantages are similar to a reinvoicing centre described previously.

Forfaiting

Forfaiting is a trade financing method that has existed for many years and has developed significantly in the last 30 years. Trading is centred in Zurich and London with primary dealers and a secondary market trading the debts. Forfaiting is the purchase of trade debt, usually at a discount, without recourse to the seller of the obligation. It is factoring without the right to collect from the previous holders of the debt if the debtor defaults. This non-recourse feature allows the debt to be tradeable, as previous holders can sell all rights and obligations.

The forfait instrument is normally a promissory note, as bills of exchange often give recourse to the drawer under local statutory regulations.

The pricing of the forfait paper depends on three factors:

1 the provision of finance;

2 the assumption of credit risk; and

3 the assumption of currency risk.

Periods of financing are usually three to five years. There is often a commitment fee charged to the original seller of the paper where there is an arrangement committing the dealer to taking forfait paper at an agreed discount rate.

It is also common for the purchaser to be selective in the debts that he is willing to buy. He may run bank credit checks on the debtors where the individual amounts are significant.

General pricing of paper is set by market conditions; interest rates and competition.

Countertrade

It might seem unusual to suggest that barter is a currency instrument, but it is the fact that the use of barter reduces the exposure to currencies. Barter often is used because of currency problems; one party to the transaction cannot obtain a currency acceptable to the other party.

Not all counter-trade is simple barter. It might be the parallel contracts of counter-purchase (see Fig 7 opposite).

Counter-purchase has the currency advantage that the currency flows are matching and therefore neutral.

Advance purchase using an escrow bank account has a similar matching currency effect (see Fig 8 opposite).

With advanced purchase the currency is not only matched but the currency flows are restricted to local bank accounts.

Inventory financing

This is another method similar to factoring. In this case it is not debts that are purchased, but the stock in trade. It gives the opportunity to settle currency amounts with the cash received. It is possible that some of the stock was held overseas and thus denominated in currency so that the sale would reduce this exposure.

Cushion pricing

Cushion pricing is margin protection by increasing a foreign currency price to a level that gives a certain sterling value, or more, whatever the exchange rate to sterling moves to. This is a simple method of FX protection but not calculated to win export orders. Marketing philosophy normally suggests that the price in a market should be what the market will bear. Cushion pricing is the sort of policy that a monopoly supplier, who was not interested in maximising his return, would use.

Currency warrants

These are warrants that are issued with bonds. For example, a US dollar Eurobond may have attached a warrant entitling the holder to buy a bond denominated in ECUs (or Deutsche Marks or Swiss francs). The investor is looking for the opportunity to buy a bond in a stronger currency if the US dollar falls in value. The investor pays for the option to purchase the strong currency bond at a fixed FX rate by receiving a lower interest return on the original bond. In some cases the investor has to hand in the original bond as part of the purchase price of the strong currency bond. This is called a harmless debt warrant, as the total debt of the issuer does not increase if the warrant is exercised.

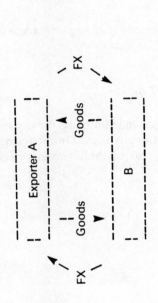

Fig 7

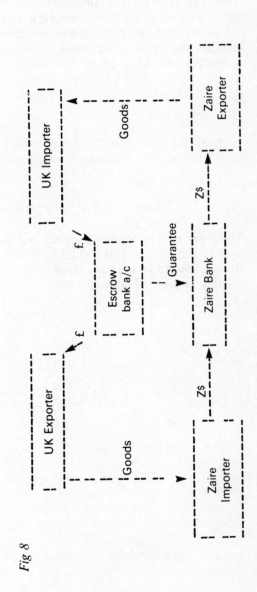

Fig 8

Convertible debt and equity warrants

There can be a currency effect with convertible debt and similar equity warrants issued with foreign currency debt. If a sterling based company issues convertible US dollar debt, the act of conversion into sterling equity from US dollar debt changes the currency exposure of the company. Harmless equity warrants would have the same effect.

Insurance

Hedging can be achieved by a commercial insurance policy in such instances as sales tendered for in foreign currency but this can be uncertain.

Bills of exchange with a 'shortfall' undertaking

These are bills in foreign currency but with clauses indemnifying the drawer against exchange loss. British exporters have traditionally traded in the former British Empire in sterling. There is a widespread fear of the uncertainties of quoting in other currencies.

DESIGNING A CURRENCY MANAGEMENT SYSTEM

SUMMARY

This chapter deals with the factors that must be included in an FX exposure management system. It continues with a suggested format for calculating and monitoring exposures.

Factors and influences

Whenever a business entity undertakes any transactions across national borders, it creates exchange exposure. This exposure represents a potential for gain or loss. Currency assets and liabilities have a fluctuating value for the business and are said to be exposed.

Whilst almost every business could export and import, the problem is of relatively minor complexity for small businesses. The level of complexity increases as a business's international trading operations grow in volume and in the number of countries dealt with. The level of complexity reaches more severe proportions for a multinational company (MNC), with the level of sophistication required in management reaching its height with the MNC conglomerate. Much has been written about hedging FX exposure, but a MNC conglomerate has special problems created by its matrix of currency relationships. The problem is collecting data on exposures in good time and different levels of risk tolerance and sensitivity in the various operating units. The exposure problems of different business types is of interest to treasurers, controllers and finance directors.

Table of FX exposure (FXE) complexity

Scale of operations	Level of FXE complexity	Sources of complexity
Small trader	None	
Small manufacturer	Erratic	Occasional imports and exports
Import/export factor	Simple and constant	Constant currency trading. Short periods of FXE. FXE often passed on to customers or suppliers.
Large manufacturer /service	Moderately complex	Large volumes but few currencies, eg raw materials
MNC	Complex	Similar to a large manufacturer but many bases.
MNC conglomerate		
Centralised (all hedged)	Moderately complex	FXE neutralised at an early stage.
Centralised (subsidiaries make some decisions)	Complex	Some FXE problems remain with the subsidiaries. Less central netting.

The role of the treasurer is as the custodian of the cash and liquid assets of the business. His management information system should generate information to enable him to:

(a) undertake day to day operations within risk parameters; and

(b) set up his deals in the context of the enterprises's strategy, investment and plans.

The importance of this type of information cannot be overrated. Any number of well respected businesses have been brought to the edge of bankruptcy by currency losses. This is often caused by the trap of borrowing a strong currency with a low interest rate to finance weak currency assets. The problem is that the FX appreciation of the strong currency against the weak is often greater than the interest differential. The borrower makes a small interest saving at the expense of a large FX loss.

A further reason for FX losses, especially by financial institutions, is FX over-trading. This is where an official authorised to trade in FX exceeds reasonable dealing volumes. He may be trying to earn profits to cover past losses or have a fraudulent motive. Financial institutions will need an extensive FX monitoring and reporting system. The system which is described in detail next, is not appropriate for that level of dealing and position taking, but would be appropriate for most businesses which were not specialist FX dealers.

It is suggested that any business which has significant FX exposures, should monitor those exposures on a regular basis. There are the various levels of exposure, transaction, translation and economic. These are discussed at length elsewhere, but each will have a different significance for a business. Management has to decide how important it considers each measure. A currency exposure forecast gives a basis on which to carry out FX exposure policy.

The forecast is structured to compute the different levels of exposure. A separate forecast sheet is produced for each currency. Management may decide that certain currencies change in value in close harmony with each other and therefore can be grouped on one forecast. This grouping decision should be reviewed regularly, in case these sympathetic movements end.

Figures are entered for the latest month for which actual currency figures are available together with forecast month end balances for each of six months into the future. Each business will need to consider whether this six-month horizon is appropriate for its activities. If it has many long-term contracts, month ends could be projected further. The forecast period should cover one complete short-term business cycle, but at the same time should not be too long to provide reliable estimates. In the Fig 9 below one ten-month exposure cycle (January to October) can be seen, although a subsequent shorter cycle appears to be forming. Management has to decide on a representative average period for cycles.

In view of the importance of cash flow information, a net cash flow exposure figure is computed on the forecast (1 on the forecast below). This is often referred to as transaction exposure and is used as such by those treasurers who lay less stress on the management of currency translation exposure, which is by their calculation the balance of total accounting exposure. Therefore, transaction plus translation exposure gives accounting exposure. There is a strong argument for limiting cash hedges to the constraints of available net cash flow, which is essentially transaction exposure. This is one reason why some treasurers only manage transaction exposure, because they only use cash instruments to hedge exposure.

The next level of exposure to be calculated, is gross asset/liability accounting exposure (2 on the forecast below). From this is deducted the value of currency hedges already transacted. This figure should be computed in terms of effective hedges, ie the net hedges which offset the assets or liabilities to be hedged. To obtain the value of a net hedge, it may well be necessary to adjust the gross hedge taken out for the taxation applicable to it. The deduction of effective

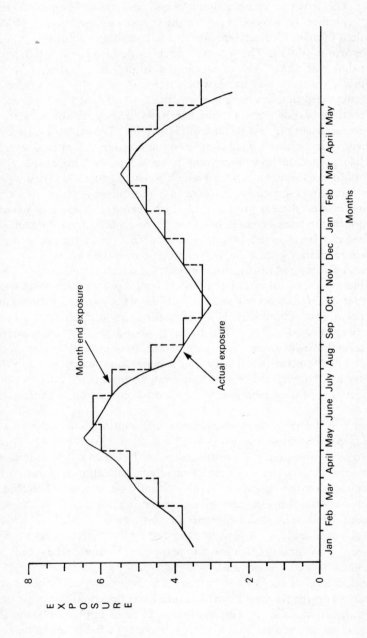

Fig 9

Currency exposure forecast

CURRENCY..................................,..........................   DATE....................

	This month end	Future months—estimated					
		Mth 1	Mth 2	Mth 3	Mth 4	Mth 5	Mth 6
Cash flows							
Cash receivables							
Receivables							
Cash hedges							
Payables							
Borrowings							
1 Net cash flow							
Balance sheet current assets							
Cash							
Receivables							
Stocks							
Investments							
Less current liabilities							
Borrowings							
Payables							
Gross liquid asset liability exposure							
Fixed assets							
Less deferred liabilities							
2 Gross asset/liability accounting exposure							
Foreign exchange contracts							
Forwards							
Options							
3 Net asset/liability accounting exposure							
Less opening net equity position in currency							
4 Profit and loss account exposure							
5 Economic influences not quantified in the accounts							
6 New hedging decisions							
Comments							

hedges gives a total accounting exposure (net asset/liability accounting exposure: 3 on the forecast above). This is the figure which eventually generates reported foreign currency exchange differences.

For those businesses reporting in the UK under accounting standard SSAP20, exchange gains and losses are split and reported in different parts of the accounts. The rules for splitting and presenting the gains and losses take up a large part of the accounting standard; they cannot be described in detail here, but there follows a very generalised summary of the methods. Exchange movements in the financial year arising on an opening foreign currency net equity investment are recorded directly in the balance sheet reserves. A foreign exchange transaction concluded as a hedge for another item is matched with that item for the purpose of accounting for foreign exchange movements. Gains and losses on all other items are included in the profit and loss account. The accounting standards of various other countries have a similar split treatment for exchange differences.

To recognise the differences in accounting treatment, the opening net equity movements are deducted from net asset-liability accounting exposure to give the gains and losses reported in the profit and loss account. Hedges of specific items will normally net out in earlier parts of the form.

Below the computed profit and loss account exposure (4 on the forecast above), is a line for currency influences which are not quantified in the accounts as exchange gains or losses (5 on the forecast above). These are influences which affect figures in the accounts other than those reported as exchange movements, or which do not appear in the accounts at all. Influences apparently as far removed as the principal production currency environment of a main competitor can have a dramatic effect on a company's profitability. Such factors are normally very difficult to quantify, but some type of periodic consideration may help to explain or forestall later 'unforeseen' losses. If a figure cannot be computed, a brief description of the factor is sufficient to remind management of its existence.

A prudent management will consider all the measures of currency exposure shown by the currency exposure forecast. Over time, relationships and the relative importance of each measure to a business will emerge and enable management to limit its detailed consideration to fewer headings. It is safest, however, if all the measures continue to be calculated in order to warn of unforeseen changes.

The reason for using month-end figures in the currency exposure forecast is for ease of calculation and availability. Actual exposure will vary during a month, but probably does not move wildly. Unlike currency values, exposures tend to be fairly static or follow stable trends. The month-end fixes give an approximate average of actual exposures, as can be seen from the graph above. Using the month-end figures gives similar movements to actuals but with half a month's lag and fewer indications of peaks and troughs. A closer average could be achieved by using the average figure for the month but this would still not show all peaks and troughs. Whether it is worth computing this forecast average month will have to be decided by individual managements. It is unusual to go to these lengths of accuracy with forecast figures.

The calculation of the amount exposed in a foreign currency is the first element of a system of foreign currency management. The exposure amounts in each currency must be reviewed in relation to the business's base currency to show their relative importance. It must be certain that the important exposure factors have been isolated. It is easy for them only to come to light when senior management suddenly notice a large loss which investigation proves to have an obscure FX basis.

The treasurer might consider forestalling the awkward questions by instituting a regular in-depth study of material currency exposures nurtured by other departments of the business. All contacts with other departments of a new type can cause political problems and have to be well thought out. If qualified and diplomatic treasury staff can be spared to work with the other departments, they will have the advantage of knowing intimately how the business works. There could, however, be some distrust on the part of other departments in having treasury people in their midst. If this is a marked factor outside help, possessing political impartiality may be preferred. The form of the investigation needs to be carefully chosen. It could be described as a currency exposure audit and must be endorsed by senior management as being important for the company. People hate being audited but are used to accepting it if it is imposed from above. Different organisations have different methods of dealing with investigation and change. They may have their own most appropriate method, such as a joint working party.

Having completed this first sweep of the business, it should be clear where the material exposures tend to arise. The treasurer has to decide how he will update the information. He cannot hope to monitor change personally in the far flung areas of generation of these exposures. He should educate his line manager colleagues so that they are aware when they change or produce a material currency exposure. He must encourage them to notify the treasury of the change. A form could be produced to supplement the monthly currency exposure forecast if that form is not tracking all the exposure information. The forecast form should show up all exposures, but in view of manager's love of forms, peripheral forms of a package are often incorrectly completed in the rush to get the package finished by the deadline. Junior staff, who do not understand all the possibilities, may also be delegated production of the forecast when a reporting department or subsidiary is under time pressure. The treasurer will have to decide when he has to send his own staff to investigate.

With the currency exposure forecast information validated, an appropriate exposure management policy can be decided upon and the necessary action, such as further hedging transactions, undertaken. Collection of extensive exposure management information may seem arduous and excessive, but any business with material currency interests has much to lose. Various surveys amongst businessmen have recorded currency volatility as their main worry concerning international trade. This concern is justifiable. In recent years the major trading currencies have averaged a 20% change in value against other currencies each year. With Bretton Woods 2 very much at an early discussion stage and quite likely not to proceed further, this volatility looks like continuing. An annual 20% change in the cost of factors of production or the revenue from turnover must be significant for a business. Management can easily justify incurring some cost to obtain data on the exposure of its business to currency movements. It is basic information that is required. It should not need to pose a threat to other managers. With a firm foundation of up-to-date information, management can proceed to frame and execute its currency exposure management policy.

TYPES OF FOREIGN CURRENCY EXPOSURE

SUMMARY

This chapter describes the different types of foreign currency exposure. Care should be exercised, as other authors may well use varying definitions for transaction, translation or economic exposure. The important thing is that you know what is in the figure you are using, not so much what it is called. There is a concluding section on bookkeeping methods for currencies.

Exposure types

Perhaps the best understood area of FX exposure is accounting exposure, as this yields the exchange gains and losses clearly recorded as such in the financial accounts of a business. The more cursory methods of FX exposure management concentrate on this measure of exposure as the effect of the actions taken reflects clearly in the financial accounts.

Accounting conventions have been the main force in recording the bulk of accounting exposure in two constituent parts. These are transactional and translational exposures. Transactional exposures arise from physical action such as a sale of goods or a foreign exchange conversion. A translational exposure is an accounting value which produces exchange differences when financial statements are produced in another currency. Translational exposures can be split into short- and long-term elements. The short-term items are those that will soon be realised and therefore will soon have a cashflow effect. Long-term items are not expected to have a cashflow effect soon. A treasurer would be less likely to cover a long-term item with a cash hedge.

The translational exposures are normally due to past transactions. Therefore a particular transaction will produce a transactional exposure in only one accounting period and thereafter will become part of translational exposure. Clearly this splitting of accounting exposure is not very precise.

Accounting standards are also responsible for different methods of subdividing the narrow definitions of accounting exposure as recorded in the books of account. Different countries have their own accounting standard setting bodies. The different methods for balance sheet and profit and loss account conversions can be summarised by the following chart:

	Closing rate	Average rate	Historic rate
Closing rate	All	—	—
Average rate	Balance sheet	P & L	—
Temporal (current /non-current)	Current assets and liabilities	—	All other
Temporal (monetary /nonmonetary	Cash, debtors and all liabilities	—	All other

In the chart the closing rate is the FX rate ruling at the end of the period under review. The average rate is an average of rates ruling throughout the period. There are various ways of calculating this average, but the important thing is that the method of calculation is consistently applied. The historic rate is the exchange rate ruling when the item first arose.

Amongst multinational companies there is currently a trend to change the method of treating foreign currencies in the profit and loss account from closing rate valuation to average rate. Opinion in UK financial circles has always been strongly in favour of the closing rate method for currency values in balance sheets. Methods which used historic values for some parts of the balance sheet and current value for others, such as the temporal systems, were considered to produce unacceptable distortions. The replacement of accounting standard FASB 8 by FASB 52 in the USA was an attempt to contain these distortions, though some would say that it did not go far enough. The appropriate valuation method for the profit and loss account has never been quite as clear.

The consensus of expert opinion in the UK supported a choice of either a closing or average rate for the profit and loss account. The USA has alway been firmly in favour of average rates.

The argument for average rates is based on the view that the profit and loss account shows results for a period and thus should have its currency values converted at a period rate. To this is added the point that the year-ends of many large businesses coincide with financial market quarter-ends (31 March, 30 June, 30 September and 31 December). These quarter-ends are often periods of exchange rate volatility caused by technical factors such as 'window dressing' and an otherwise thin market.

Support for the closing rate method stems from the view that the balance sheet is best converted at the closing rate and the profit and loss account supplies part of the movement in revenue reserves and must be in sympathy with the rest of the accounts. There is the further argument that unremitted profits should have a current valuation, as this is the most up-to-date approximation of their value when they are finally remitted. Such an argument, however, would equally support an after-year-end rate of valuation and hence is rather impractical.

It would be good to think that these arguments were the main considerations influencing people in major companies in their choice of which currency valuation method to adopt for their profit and loss account. Unfortunately this is unlikely to be so.

For instance, in 1985 sterling steadily strengthened aginst the US dollar so that the dollar earnings of sterling-based companies were depressed. A number of such companies were unhappy with the closing rate valuation highlighting this. They conveniently ignored the fact that the closing rate method had magnified the sterling value of dollar profits in years of falling sterling rates. They firmly resolved to change from the closing rate valuation to an average rate. They should take a long-term view where accounting policies are concerned. A change in one year may improve reported results but may not serve their purpose in subsequent years.

Accounting for FX translation differences

	SSAP 20 (UK)	FASB 52 (USA)	IAS 21 (World)
Profit and loss account	Average or closing	Average	Average or closing
Opening net worth of subs	Not shown separately	Shown separately	Not shown separately
Disclosure	Unnecessary for P and L. Disclose accounting policy	Necessary for P and L	Unnecessary for P and L. Disclose accounting policy

It was pointed out earlier that the the US standard FASB 52 was produced to simplify the situation after the previous standard, FASB 8. However, in one way it produces a new complication. Transaction and translation exposure are given revised definitions. A central currency has to be chosen for each business unit. This is the currency of the environment in which the business operates and is termed the functional currency. The decision as to the relevant currency in each case is that of management and they have some latitude in this. For the purposes of FASB 52, any conversion of currencies into the functional currency produces transactional exchange differences, whilst conversion of currencies from the functional currency into another currency for reporting financial statements produces translational exchange differences.

The UK accounting standard SSAP 20 varies from FASB 52 in the following ways:

1   SSAP 20 allows closing rate profit and loss conversion in addition to average rate.

2   FASB 52 is stricter in defining currencies which can be recorded as a hedge for another item.

3   FASB 52 only allows a recorded hedge for a subsidiary investment.

4   Hyper-inflation country subsidiaries should be accounted for by the temporal method for FASB 52. SSAP 20 requires inflation adjusted figures converted at closing rates.

5   FASB 52 requires separate profit and loss account disclosure of exchange gains and losses. SSAP 20 does not.

6   FX adjustments, passed directly through reserves, have to be disclosed separately each year and as a carried forward balance for FASB 52. For SSAP 20, only the current year's adjustment need be shown separately.

7   For FASB 52 if a subsidiary is sold any accumulated exchange differences that were taken direct to reserves, must be passed through the profit and loss account. SSAP 20 does not require this.

The international accounting standard No 21 is similar but broader than FASB 52 and SSAP 20. Therefore any business applying either of the latter two accounting standards will automatically comply with the international standard.

From the descriptions so far it will be clear that whether an exchange profit or loss is realised or unrealised is not important for the accounting standards of the UK, US or the international body. There are countries where the distinction is still important, such as West Germany. In such countries unrealised exchange profits are not taken to the profit and loss account until they become realised.

It is clear that there is a fair degree of latitude allowed in the calculation and presentation of foreign currency gain and loss items. For instance, the international standard and the UK standard allow closing rate exchange rate valuation or historic rate valuation for non-monetary assets. The differing treatments can produce quite different results in the financial accounts. For this reason it is essential that there should be some consistency in the translation treatment adopted by any one company. If a company is allowed freely to vary its translation treatment it has the power to manipulate its financial accounts for short-term gain.

Economic exposure

Apart from recorded accounting currency exposure, there is an element of foreign currency exposure which does not readily show up in the accounts of an enterprise. It is not that it does not affect the accounts, just that it does not appear as an exchange difference. An example of this type of exposure is an asset or liability accounted for in one currency, but with an underlying value in another currency. A German company might quote a sterling price but adjust that price in relation to its Deutsche Mark costs. These Deutsche Mark fluctuations would be absorbed in purchases in the accounts. Another type of hidden exposure is pricelist exposure. If a business has issued a pricelist to an overseas market with foreign currency prices, this immediately produces an exposure. Orders can be placed at these prices at any time but an accounting exposure only arises when a sale is recorded.

As these effects are masked there is the danger that they are disregarded by management. Difficulties in collecting this more obscure data has meant that it was largely ignored or dismissed on cost-benefit grounds. Any method of monitoring currency fluctuations and their effect on business, must take into account such masked effects. Attention is often only focused when a large reported loss is proved to be caused by currency movements and senior management ask the treasury department for an explanation. Bland statements such as 'they do not emanate from the treasury department' or 'we ignore non-accounting currency exposures' may not satisfy or impress.

Some of these economic exposures are long-term factors. Alternatively management may consider that real exposure only occurs when legal title passes. Most treasury specialists would find this attitude difficult to justify as much can happen to currency values before legal title passes.

The effect of variable exchange rates on reported financial results, when there may be no real exposure to currency movements but the timing of income recognition can produce unreal currency gains or losses. This is an accounting problem with major implications for management.

Bookkeeping methods

There are two basic methods of recording currencies in the books of a business. Either all currencies are recorded at their value in the base currency, say sterling for a UK company, or multicurrency books of account are set up. In multicurrency books each currency has a separate ledger which is balanced using a clearing or buffer account. Any transaction across currencies would appear in the buffer account of both currencies. Below is an example of journal entries to record an FX deal.

EXAMPLE.   Spot FX transaction to sell £1 million for $1.5 million.

	Debit	Credit
Sterling ledger		
Buffer account	1m	
Cash at bank account		1m
US dollar ledger		
Cash at bank account	1.5m	
Buffer account		1.5m

As can be seen from this example, the buffer account shows the exposure in the currency. If all cross-currency transactions are put through the buffer account, then the balance on that account will show the net accounting exposure for that currency.

The books of account for a multinational business should be kept on a multicurrency system as it allows accounting exposure figures to be easily extracted from the balances on the buffer accounts. There should be efficiencies in having one set of books of account that yields sufficient control information for the treasury, management accounting and statutory accounting. This will save input costs and give homogeneous information to all users of the accounting system. Treasury or other management can demand the accounting system to produce the subdivisions of the exposure that they require, but should not get too misled by the importance of subdivisions of accounting exposure. They must bear in mind any significant economic exposures that the accounting exposure figure does not contain.

POLICY METHODS

SUMMARY

This chapter deals with the policy decisions to be taken. It starts with the key decision on centralised or decentralised management. Further decisions have to then be made to control all aspects of the department. There is a discussion on the way banks use dealing limits. These could have a wider application by corporations than they have at present. After a section on risk calculation, the final part of the chapter deals with FX mandates and swap agreements.

Policy

Whether a multinational should manage currency fluctuation problems on a centralised or decentralised basis has long been a bone of contention. It is argued that a centralised system can become too insensitive to local needs and conditions (Earl, 1985, Allen, 1985), but generally a substantial element of centralisation is accepted as the best method (Brooke and Remmers, 1978). At least the framework of strategy and policy should be determined by the central treasury (Hodson, 1985). It is possible for a central treasury to buy the FX exposures of the divisions at an economic or market price. Then the central treasury is in a position to net complimentary flows and to deal in bulk. It is more cost effective to have a group's treasury expertise in one place. As the exposures are bought from the divisions at a market price, there should be no cause for complaint from them.

Elements of the far-flung risk must not be missed. Ford Germany suffered a warehouse fire which was insured by a captive US insurance company. Between the loss and the settlement of the claim, a further 50% currency loss was suffered as the pending claim was not recognised as a currency exposure (Reier, 1984).

A divisionalised organisation which has delegated currency exposure decisions to divisional heads, may at the same time have highly centralised divisions (Child, 1984). Management must decide on the appropriate devolvement.

Businesses can also be classified in another way.

1 Ethnocentric – based on the country of origin.
2 Polycentric – based on each host country.
3 Geocentric – supranational management having allegiance only to the business headquarters.

An internationally-based treasury is more likely to occur in polycentric and geocentric businesses. The neutrality and autonomy of a worldwide enterprise should allow fewer restrictions on the FX management activities. If the management decision centre is very much one-country based, it can suffer all the restrictions of that country plus those of the country involved in a particular consideration.

In framing policy, management ethos also has to be considered. The desired risk to reward ratio and the degree of interest in managing FX positions will be significant. If the prevailing view is conservative and the idea is put forward that the company's aim is to manufacture its main product with other areas neutralised not managed, then such a company would hedge all exposures possible. If the company's view is to pick up revenue and cost saving from wherever it can, then active management of its FX position will be considered. For instance, the Geneva FX dealing room of French car-maker Renault is larger than that of many banks. The Renault example gives another facet of management ethos in that as a nationalised concern, it professes not to speculate against the French franc despite remunerative opportunities to do so. The major French banks are also nationalised and may well exercise similar self-restraint.

Business is all about making important decisions concerning scarce resources and their allocation. Since enterprise exists in an environment of risk, FX is no different from other risks. Any policy has to determine the nature of the phenomenon and the ways in which it can be handled. Three fundamental principles are involved.

1 Identification. In a dynamic productive process new and varied risks emerge. Discovery is an essential precursor to action.

2 Measurement. Likelihood and severity of the occurrence.

3 Control. The efficient means of dealing with the risk.

Risk can be generally classified as follows:

(a) Speculative and pure risk – occurring from unfortunate managerial decisions, political factors and changes in technology.

(b) Fundamental and particular risk – uncertainties, inaccuracies and disharmonies in the economic system.

(c) Insurable and non-insurable risk – insurability (hedging in the case of FX) requires probabilistic predictability, fortuitousness and definable chance of loss.

In deciding on the means of framing an FX policy, it is important not to make the method too difficult to follow. This is a danger with using the theoretical risk subdivisions above and from using involved mathematics. Some possible methods are not simple enough to prompt the serious attention and interest of FX management. Recent writers have developed very complex models without regard to the average qualifications of the majority of practitioners or the extent of the information, facilities and time available to complete their jobs. Such theories will continue to have a limited audience in the business world.

Treasurers are more concerned with identifying FX risk. This is down to simple eyes, ears, imagination and shoe leather. Systematic methods of finding risk such as an 'exposure meter' questionnaire may not be excessive and are certainly simple.

The simple rules of risk management are:

1 Do not risk more than you can afford to lose.

2 Do not risk much for little.

3 Consider the odds.

The risk control techniques are:

(a) Risk avoidance – limit currency use from the outset.

(b) Risk assumption – decide to bear some of the currency risk. The potential loss against the strength of the business must be weighed.

(c) Risk transfer – sell the risk to someone else as cheaply as possible.

(d) Hedging – arranging to offset the FX risk. Risk is a fundamental part of business. It is a continual exercise in decision-making under uncertainty.

Those involved in policy decisions

The intellectual resources of the business must be mobilised. Management time is expensive and in short supply, but currency management is an important topic. It is not just the domain of treasurers, accountants or finance people in general. Many departments will suffer if the wrong decisions are made, so other departments should be involved from the outset. All managers should be alive to all risks, not just their particular discipline.

A regularly meeting 'currency committee' is a good way of framing the general treasury policy for FX. As a minimum the committee should consist of the finance director, treasurer, chief accountant, tax manager and the chief FX dealer. If members of other departments are not included on the committee, they should submit reports to it and receive copies of its minutes. The sales department and the purchasing department ought to be included as they will suffer if there is indequate FX management and have much to gain from good FX management.

The FX dealers would carry out the decisions of the committee and would confer with the treasurer in the event of changed circumstances and obvious conflicts. The treasurer would also have the power to intervene if he considers that the committee's decisions are no longer appropriate.

File committee meetings would aim to achieve the following:

1 Assimilate outside currency views collected by the treasurer from banks and professional forecasters.

2 Spread currency awareness around decision-making areas of the business.

3 Constantly review dealing policies to be in step with the market and to try to detect future trends.

4 Encourage in-house forecasts to be produced and constructively commented upon.

5 Advise divisions on current FX problems.

6 Refer problems to the tax or legal specialists immediately it is necessary to do so.

7 Review instances when limits imposed on dealings are exceeded.

The point about limits is interesting. Bank dealing operations have extensive dealing control systems using limits. These systems have not featured nearly so strongly in corporate treasury. This is mainly because most corporate treasuries have not traded their positions, so that there was little need for control. As more positions are taken there will be more need for a system of limits similar to those used by banks.

Limits do not only relate to FX risk, but the whole range of limits is considered here as to do otherwise might be confusing. Different types of limits often need to work together in order to be effective.

The idea of limits is that a maximum figure is computed for safe exposure to any one type of risk. The figure may be set as the maximum loss the management are willing too suffer for that risk or it might be set by some external rule or regulation which has to be complied with.

A broad structure of limits would consist of:

1 counterparty credit limits;

2 capacity limits;

3 sovereign limits;

4 currency limits;

5 liquidity limits;

6 delivery limits; and

7 interest-rate limits.

In addition to this subdivision there would also be a higher overall level for limits during dealing hours (daylight limits) rather than those applying for longer periods. This is based on the assumption that short-term risk can have less effect than long-term risk as quick switches from one item at risk to another should have more of an evening effect.

Limits can also be split between advisory and essential. Daylight limits might be advisory, as exceeding them in a minor way should not be that damaging. Overnight limits could be classed as essential, because they relate to a period of currency movement which is not controlled by the business as the dealing room is closed for the night. An excessive position overnight could accumulate large losses. In practical terms, the authorisation of increases in limit amounts should be much more difficult to obtain for essential limits.

Counter-party credit limits

Counter-party credit limits are required to protect the dealer from excessive loss in the event of default by the counter-party to a transaction. If it is a complex transaction there may be many counter-parties and the risk of each principal party must be assessed. Where a counter-party is acting as an agent, consideration must be given to the practicality of taking action against his principal if necessary. If it is impractical to take action against the principal, the agent's creditworthiness has to be considered. Depending on the size and frequency of dealing, different methods of assessing risk will be used.

For occasional small customers, management experience, with no outside help, may be used as the basis. For large or frequent customers, some outside help should be used. For well known corporates one of the stock market rating or information services could be used. It would be presumed that they were a good risk, so that the search would be fairly routine. For less well known organisations, a bank reference and review of available accounts and other information is advisable. The cost in time and money must be weighed against the possible loss. When the information is obtained, it may not be completely reliable. It is not worth the effort of investigating the chance of an insignificant loss. On the other hand, considerable investigation into the chance of a major loss is worthwhile.

It has to be remembered that the credit risk in FX dealing is normally a margin risk, not a full capital risk as with a loan. The possible loss on say a forward deal is that the counter-party defaults and the deal has to be closed out in the current forward market for the original maturity. The possible loss is the difference between the original forward price and that obtained to close out the deal (the result might be a profit, but it is unlikely that a counter-party would default on a valuable forward). The full capital risk only occurs at the delivery stage (see delivery limits described later).

Capacity limits

Capacity limits relate to the total of risk that an undertaking can assume. The calculation starts with a search for the statutory and regulatory limitations on the enterprise. It may be that there are borrowing limits in the formation charter of the organisation. This might be a proportion of capital or assets or it might be a set figure. If the business is under some form of government control, there may be stated financial maximums of various types. Banks are perhaps the main sufferers from government regulation, but other organisations such as public utilities will often also be constrained in some way.

In addition to limits imposed from outside, there will be limits for risk that management decides upon. This may be partly to take into account outside opinions on the business. Investment analysts, journalists and remote shareholders may be unhappy if certain levels of risk are exceeded. The main consideration will be, however, what management consider the business can safely risk. It could be argued that even here management impose such a limitation to avoid the chance of being sacked by irate owners of the business following a catastrophic loss.

Once the total limit has been set, it is then subdivided into levels for each control area. This subdivision is important. It is all too easy to leave unused limit available in one area, whilst another area has to constrain profitable business because it has reached its allocated maximum limit. It is often best to have some means of allowing one area to transfer, perhaps on a temporary basis, some part of its capacity limit. This method might also be useful for other types of limits where rigid subdivision is used.

Many banks over-allocate capacity limits to the control areas, in the knowledge that all areas will not use up their allocation and the overall limit will not be exceeded. This is akin to the loan funding principle that you can lend more than you hold as cash, as you will never be asked to pay all loans out as cash. Such a method saves the administration of surrendering limit from one area to another.

Capacity limits have to take into account the fact that most FX risk is only on the margin between contracted and current market price. Only delivery risk is at the full capital value and this is a very short-term risk.

Sovereign limits

Sovereign limits relate to the risk of a foreign country imposing limitations on the business. The restrictions might not relate to payment of a debt, but this is normally the main concern. There may not be an embargo on payment, it could be that a regulation is passed that reduces the value of the payment by, say, instituting a multiple-rate exchange rate with some payment at a worse rate. Often the sovereign risk is assessed with counter-party risk, but this would be wrong if the counter-party trades from various countries with very different characteristics. It may be that the counter-party is forced to default by regulation in the country concerned and would not feel duty bound to make good the loss from his resources in other countries.

The well known countries at risk are those that have suffered from the debt crisis or the oil shocks. It must be remembered that the countries at risk in the past may not be the ones at risk in the future. The old debtors may be eager to please creditors and a comparatively good risk. The real problem is the country about to destabilise: the revolution, years of corruption or just bad luck with the price weakness of primary exports. The extent to which you become an international economist and political expert depends on the limit of the risk to your business. Will it help to say that you cannot be expected to prophesy international events when half your major export debts go bad? Such an opinion is more defensible if you only lose the value of a few small shipments.

Currency limits

The currency limit might be considered to be the most important limit, because losses from exchange can occur more often than, say, through credit bad debts. The risk assessment has some connection with the assessment of the country risk of the country responsible for the currency, but currency risk goes further. A perfectly sound country could have a very volatile currency. Currency limits have to be set by the use of a broad estimate of the volatility of each currency and the maximum loss sustainable. More volatile currencies do not have to have smaller limits. Dealers may want to take positions in the volatile currencies in order to make exchange gains. To limit dealers to very stable currencies is to limit severely their opportunity to make such gains. The total volatilities of all currencies traded have to be contained by the limits.

A currency limit system should have three parts:

1 a gross long position limit (total currency assets);

2 a gross short position limit (total currency liabilities); and

3 a net position limit (the net of assets and liabilities).

It is necessary to have gross and net constituents, as a small net position may conceal large long and short elements which do not offset in all respects. This point about gross and net limits relates to other limit types as well.

It is important that a deal is recorded against the true currency of exposure. The declared nominal currency of the instrument may not be the currency which fundamentally affects it. However, given that the limits are used against a constantly changing trading position, there are practical problems to such deep analysis in all but the most common examples. A decision has to be taken as to whether the materiality of such a re-classification makes it worthwhile.

Liquidity limits

The liquidity limit seeks to ensure that a business is not short of liquid funds when they are needed. This is basically a cash management problem but also safeguards flows of currencies when these are needed. Most businesses would have sources of currency funds ready for urgent need, so that liquidity limits are needed only as a disaster backup. Consequently they would be set at a very broad level, which is is just as well because their precise application is perhaps difficult.

Liquidity or maturity risk is most easily shown on a gap report or ladder. This is a report that shows maturities in chronological order, with or without totals and subtotals. These reports are easy to produce but not very easy to interpret. It is difficult to institute a computerised monitoring system or apply a single value limit.

In order to monitor the liquidity risk with a single value limit it is necessary to translate the total maturity information into one index number per control area. Changes in the profile of maturities changes this number. The equation producing the number could be structured to give a low number for a good liquidity profile and a high number for a bad liquidity profile. With this calculation being made after each portfolio change, the new number is compared with a stated maximum. If the maximum is exceeded an alarm bell is sounded in the system and a detailed assessment takes place to see what is undesirable in the position; the number itself would not directly give the reason, it is just a warning.

The types of equation used have evolved over a number of years. Some 15 years ago a standard model was produced which was amended five years ago to take account of shortcomings when portfolio values changed. The latest form is the duration gap model which further seeks to cover peculiarities of a portfolio. All these models are still too simple in many ways and assume stable future trends. Some of the US banks have very sophisticated models which include assumptions on future yields and volatility.

This index number method would in practice also be used to monitor interest rate risk, as this is another factor to which it is difficult to give a single value. There would be one compound index method to warn against liquidity and interest rate problems.

Liquidity risk limits may also be used to split trading holdings and investment holdings. A limit can be set to notify when a trading holding of a currency is becoming long term and perhaps ought either to be regarded as an investment or unwound. The two definitions can have differing tax effects and therefore can be important.

Delivery limits

All FX transactions at some point require delivery of some form of value through a clearing system. Any movement of funds contains an element of risk. The banking system is geared to make so many receipts and payments with little trouble, it is easy to forget that there is a risk and that the risk can be for the full capital value of the FX deal.

Transmission systems have their own built-in security. Private telephone lines with locked switching equipment housing is now commonplace. Hardware can have its own unique reference code for others to recognise it by. Encryption of messages or a cypher number included with the message are standard for transfers, although voice recognition as an authorisation for transfers is slow to be completely superseded by corporates.

The cypher number system was originally used to authenticate telex funds transfer instructions, but it can be used for other communication methods. The system takes various elements that are needed in a transfer and codes each of them. These code numbers are then added to a set user key number and often a sequential number. The resulting compound number contains the basic elements of the transfer instruction, so that any subsequent changes to these elements, fraudulent or otherwise, will be obvious. The cypher is therefore a very good method of safeguarding transfer instructions which have to be transmitted on an open (unprotected) communications system. Manual calculation of a cypher is arduous, but it is possible to do it by machine. The cypher table or the machine program has to be held securely as it could easily be used to make fraudulent payments.

If all these security measures are used, there should be a greatly diminished delivery risk, but still a risk exists. Banks are not infallible and some are weaker than many big corporations as far as credit risk is concerned. Consideration must be given to the value of funds which can safely be allowed to flow through the system. It is not suggested that there is a concern with anything other than very large sums, but some high level should be set for reference. Any transfer which entails bearer documents or cash, will entail a much higher degree of risk and will require lower delivery limits.

The full capital value of an FX deal is at risk when the different currencies of the deal are delivered in different time zones. The party that has to deliver in the first time zone is at full value risk until the matching payment is made in the later time zone. Delivery risk is still sometimes called Herstatt risk after a German bank Herstatt, that defaulted in 1974. Herstatt defaulted after collecting funds in the European time zone but before making payments due in US dollars in the later US time zone.

The only way to cover against this risk in cases of doubt, is to delay payment against proof of receipt of the other currency. This will lead to a penalty interest payment, but it may be worth it for the added security.

Interest rate limits

Interest rate limits do not have much to do with FX except in that the forward FX rate is a function of differential interest rates so that forward rate exposure is interest rate risk. However, a brief description is necessary for completeness. In a similar way to liquidity limits, a gap report can easily be produced but is not so easy to interpret. The index number method gives an absolute number that can be matched against the set control criteria. The interest rate and liquidity factors are normally controlled in one index number system to save calculation.

Principal sum at risk

There needs to be a definite policy on what is considered to be the capital amount at risk for particular FX instruments. The nominal principal sum for the transaction may not be the amount at risk. An illustration of a complicated calculation can be seen in the following currency swap exposure estimate.

Example

In this five-year currency swap the bank receives Danish krone at 14% per annum on a principal sum of DKK100 m. The bank has to pay fixed rate sterling, which presently costs 13% per annum. The interest rate risk factor for DKK is −3 to +4% and for sterling is +/− 2%. The present spot FX rate for GBP/DKK is 10.50 and the future rate volitility is considered to be +/− 14% reducing with time. All figures are approximate and calculated as at the beginning of the year.

Date in Years	Cash flow DKKm	(i) Rough NPV @ 14−3%	(ii) FX rate	(i/ii) NPV in £ £m	(iii) NPV of £ stream @ 13+2% £m	(i/ii-iii) Deemed exposure £m	Deemed exposure % principal
1	14	110	10.5	10	9	1	11%
2	14	108	9.0	12	10	2	18%
3	14	106	7.5	14	10	4	30%
4	14	104	6.5	16	10	6	39%
5	114	102	6.0	17	10	7	42%

Such a calculation gives the exposure in each year and the maximum exposure of the instrument. It is arguable whether the particular exposure shown for the year should be used for that year, or whether the maximum exposure should be used in each year as the most conservative policy.

Mandates and swap agreements

A policy has to be formulated as to acceptable contents of FX dealing agreements that a business is required to complete. It is first worth considering whether the business wants to adopt its own standard form document and insist on using this. The standard form has the following advantages:

1 all counterparties are dealt with on the same basis; and

2 it is easy to remember the terms on which dealings take place and there are not surprises in the small print.

Whether a standard dealing agreement can be imposed depends on the commercial power of the business.

FX dealing mandates are unusual because most banks do not wish to impede credit-worthy customers from dealing by throwing bureaucratic form-filling in the way. Dealing limits for a customer are often agreed with the minimum of effort by the customer.

Swap agreements are not quite as easy, as swaps last for five to ten years and very large margins between contract rate and current market value can build up. Acceptable clauses will be a matter of negotiation in each case. It is as well to resist being bound by cross-default, negative pledge or even pari passu clauses as problems with other agreements might then affect the swap agreement. The objective with all negotiation is to obtain the most cover whilst conceding the least to the other party. Negotiate from a position of strength.

DEALING ROOM METHODS

SUMMARY

This chapter covers transaction methods and layouts. The description of methods extends to the backoffice to give more complete picture. Bad dealing administration can cripple a treaury. You are only as good as your backoffice.

The dealing sequence

The start of the process is a 'things to do' list maintained by the dealer. This will show all the deals that he is expecting to do that day. Examples of entries would be:

1 maturing forward deals;

2 debtors due to pay; and

3 creditors expecting payment.

When a dealer transacts a deal it must be quickly recorded. If there is a machine dealing system he would probably input direct into the system. Any errors would be corrected later. If there is a manual system, a dealing slip would be completed with similar information to that input into a machine dealing system. Such a slip is illustrated in Fig 10 below.

Fig 10

```
BOUGHT/SOLD          No. FX 87–12345
Date: 5 Jan 87
To: Bank of Iceland
    London
Amount: £2,000,000
Rate: 1.50
Value: 7 Jan 87
Through: A Broker Ltd
US$ Amount: $3,000,000
Deliver to: A Clearer Plc London
For a/c: Bk Iceland FX
Funds from: First Bank Ny
    Initial boxes
    Dealer        Checked         Entered
```

A computerised dealing system

Speedy input is necessary so that the dealing position can be quickly updated. If the backoffice system is slow it is normal for the dealers to have their own system of reporting positions. A junior dealer will have a manual or small-scale computer system for quick results. It is clear that there is an element of duplication in both producing the dealing position. It could be said that one system will act as a check on the other, but reconciliation of differences will not be all that easy and there are better ways of validating system output than duplicating the whole thing. The ultimate objective is to speed up the primary backoffice system so that it can supply the dealers quickly with position totals.

The primary dealing system should be a multi-user system so that consolidations of various dealer's positions and results can be obtained. The chief dealer should be able to log into any part of the system to look at detail or to see overall totals. This should help in his task of overall control. Care should be taken that two separate dealers cannot change a single position at the same time, as this can lead to erroneous decisions by the dealer and a good chance that the machine will incorrectly process the input. The normal method of ensuring against inputs at the same time, is to assign each position to one dealer. This dealer would be given the responsibility for making certain that only one update was taking place at a time. There could also be an internal machine safeguard to allow the first person to input exclusive access to change a position until he has finished his input. Thereby, there should not be the same need to limit access to any one position at any one time. The machine should be able to cope with revising consolidated position totals as each position changes. This lessens the chance of a wrong decision being taken on the basis of an incomplete update of consolidated totals.

The information should be checked for validity at every conceivable opportunity. Parameters can be put into the system so that it can detect peculiar and therefore probably wrong data. There should also be the facility to show as much of the information in overall totals as possible. The reason for this is that if such totals become obviously wrong, these will trigger a check. Restatement of information may trigger a human response to a mistake which was not noticed in its original form.

Another useful sub-routine that can be put in the dealing system is a calender of valid dealing days for currencies. This requires a periodic update of a standing data calender with the known bank holidays. This subsystem will also have to decide how many currencies the deal will pass through and hence which holidays affect the transaction. For instance, most FX deals are based on the US dollar even if the dollar is not one of the currencies bought or sold. A sterling to Deutsche Mark FX deal with a French bank would be affected by New York holidays. The only way around this would be to deal with a British or German bank which was running its own book in the other currency.

The dealing system should also generate a confirmation letter or telex to be sent to the counter-party. At the time the deal is put into the system a suggested confirmation with pre-stored contacts and addresses could be shown to the operator for approval or amendment. It is important that confirmation be sent out as soon as possible to pick up any possible errors from an independent source.

The main output of the system for the dealing room will be revised positions for all currencies and how close the position is to the maximum dealing limits. It is best if this information is available on the dealers' internal dealing screen.

Output from the dealing system will also pass through to the backoffice. This direct link will save the monotonous paper input and checking that has so long been necessary in a backoffice. Now the backoffice staff has more of a validation role before the information is passed into the main accounting system.

The dealing desk (see Fig 11)

There is no standard layout for a dealing desk but there is a trend towards more electronic support features being built into the desk. It is considered that many of the modern desks have more features than a dealer could ever use. It is probable that the dealer is just one step behind the latest available feature and thus is stretched to keep improving his expertise. Certainly many of the older features are now indispensable to the dealer and there is no reason to think that this trend will stop.

The dealing desks are traditionally set in rows facing each other, but this is now often changed to small circles or angular designs. It is an attempt not to look too formal yet still be close together for effective dealing and monitoring what is going on. Banks of telexes and quiet meeting rooms are often sited around the edge of the room.

Fig 11

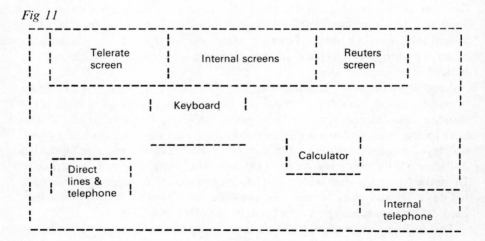

TREASURY SERVICES

SUMMARY

This chapter addresses the increasing number of services open to a treasury department. Most of them are microcomputer based. There are brief reviews of corporate treasury workstation programs, large FX dealing systems, information services and multicurrency ledger systems. The reviews have been compiled on the basis of information published by the suppliers. Some of the reviews are longer than others, but this is not an indication of greater advantages over other systems for any one application. As there are nearly 80 systems described in this chapter, the author has been involved in actually running only a small proportion. Therefore no responsibility can be taken for the details given, even though every effort has been made to ensure their accuracy.

Computerisation

As was previously noted, netting systems are generally operated on a computer system. This is because they require a large amount of simple figure processing which is an ideal application for a computer. Other aspects of exposure management also benefit from computerisation, although the process is often less easy to mechanise. Such benefits derived are as follows:

1 Speed, a very important attribute in the fast changing foreign exchange market. This is often the principal reason for mechanisation of a dealing system.

2 Accuracy, vital with the large sums of money involved.

3 Labour saving, not necessarily a decisive factor.

4 Easy interface with computer systems in other areas of a business.

5 Simple collection of exposure data from foreign subsidiaries.

6 Supplying up-to-the-minute FX rates from systems like Reuters, Telerate, Quotron and Datastream.

Software packages are available that seek to automate the dealing system or that adjust for the changes in exposures and positions after a day's dealing. The dealing system is essentially a method by which a business decides upon and reacts to FX and other treasury deals (such as borrowing/lending needs). For FX this would be spot contracts, forwards, futures, options and the numerous other FX instruments that blossom and fade as the market vogue. A number of packages fulfil the needs of the corporate treasurer and a larger number of packages serve the needs of banks and financial institutions. The packages do not give instant answers, there is normally a 10% element of customisation required (Cowe, 1985). In addition to a deal record and calculation system, a business requires some kind of system to calculate its FX exposure. Some systems simply extract currency totals from the accounting ledgers. This will not reveal some types of exposure, but management may consider that the cost of searching further outweighs the benefit. A comprehensive exposure gathering system is expensive and extensive: cost/benefit must always be borne in mind. Added to this is the fact that many companies have a backlog of projects for their data processing department (Cluff, 1985). Systems based on multiple microcomputers, seem to offer a flexible solution. Systems normally have three modules, modelling, transaction support and reporting, although this subdivision may not be clear because the package appears to be subdivided as FX, cash management and core accounting. This latter structure is shown to be more familiar to corporate treasurers. There are a number of benefits which would be of use in serving FX needs that could be provided by a corporate treasury workstation computer system.

1 Easy input, if only through single input, is one great advantage. If the first input is rigorously checked, there is a good basis for subsequent processing. Larger bank systems use input in two parts to speed initial entry and to check basic details. For any transaction there is a first input of the main details soon after the deal is agreed. Later there is another input of the rest of the details of the deal. This second input gives a chance to check the basic details.

2 Built-in checks to avoid errors. A system can include a number of subtle checks and balances which need not impede the user but will find errors before they have expensive consequences.

3 Break down composite deals into their straightforward elements. Many of the latest financial instruments are made up of, or similar to, the old basic FX transactions. A currency future is a forward deal transacted on a futures exchange. The computer system should be able to consolidate differing instruments to produce net effects.

4 Speed of processing and access. The machine should have adequate data storage and processing capability so that updates are quick and all live data is quickly accessible.

5 Performance of dealers and deal types can be assessed. The overall success of a dealer's activities can be gauged for, say, salary appraisals. Alternatively the profit or loss or dealing in a particular instrument might be needed to decide whether to continue dealing in that instrument, if past performance is considered as a good indication of what will arise in the future.

6 Bank and other counter-party performance. A computer system can log and

analyse dealings with any one counter-party. Information such as number of deals per period and average amount can indicate how valuable the relationship is for both parties. A sudden dip in volumes might indicate a change in attitude which requires investigation and action. Details of volumes are also important for bank charge negotiations as significant FX volumes can be used as a reason for lower overall charges.

7 Variances between actual and forecast results. A wide range of comparison reports can be quickly produced by a computer system.

8 Revaluations of currencies can be speedily produced so that say daily market to market revaluations of the currency portfolio would not impede the normal running of the system. By this means the cost of holding FX positions can be highlighted at an early stage and strategy changes decided upon.

9 Identification and monitoring of exposures in each currency. Detailed forms per currency and summary forms with a number of currencies shown. Different types of exposure (transaction, translation and economic) can also appear on one form.

10 Formats that show exposures, any hedges taken out and how effective these hedges are before and after tax.

11 Compliance with authorisation when deals are undertaken. The system can require authorisation by senior staff for deals above a certain level. Limits can be applied to curtail or prevent types of deal or excessive amounts. The system can report on whether these limitations are being observed.

12 Monitoring of dealing spreads and other FX costs. The system can collect such information on a routine basis, although it might only report it on an exception basis or when requested by the user.

13 Greater security is afforded for FX settlement. The word settlement is used here because a computer system can seldom put much constraint on the dealing system, unless all dealings are by electronic means. However, the backoffice operations can be given a greater level of protection with a well structured and run system. Given the very large sums of money involved such security is important, but it must be remembered that security is only as good as the weakest link in the system. It is no good having a carefully controlled main system if there is an emergency system which breaks the rules and can be used for fraud.

These points are suggestions for inclusion in a system and are in no way essential to its successful operation. Whether a user requires each of the headings depends on his individual needs.

An example of a corporate treasury system – ETS

The Econintel ETS system appears as a modular approach to treasury management but operates from a core multi-company multi-currency ledger. The system can cope with FX, moneymarket, payments, balance reporting and accounting.

Dealers have formatted input screens for rapid transaction input and have access to cash, currency and bank positions whenever they need them. The system can dial into external services for balance reporting, making payments, or obtaining FX rates. There is an optional autodial facility for, say, overnight collection of balance information.

The system is highly automated as regards confirmation letters, payment instructions and advices to counter-parties. The standard parts of the documents are taken from files of standing details and the transaction information is taken from the deal entries on the system. All that is required is a manual screen review before they are printed and sent. Such a saving of backoffice labour is very valuable in time and effort.

The system enters transactions in its own multicurrency ledger and can produce accounts that comply with the UK accounting standard (SSAP20) or the US standard (FAS 52).

There are 120 different report formats which can be viewed on a screen or printed out. Reports are selected by a series of menus. Examples are cashflow forecasts, dealing diaries, account movements, FX exposure, FX profits and losses, maturity ladders, interest accruals, limit utilisation and turnover analysis. All the normal accounting reports can be produced; daybooks, ledgers, trial balance and final accounts. Machine sensible output can be used to enter onto spreadsheet programs and to post further books of account if these are kept. The ledger package is quite adequate to produce a full set of books of account so long as all the transactions of the business can be put through the system. If the business had a substantial number of non-treasury transactions, this might not be practical.

System security is served by data backup every night and access to the system is protected by passwords linked to user account numbers. There can be restrictions on who can perform certain activities or use specific areas of the package. A comprehensive audit trail is maintained so that even deleted items can be examined if necessary.

The system is currently available to run on Digital Equipment Corporation mini and supermicro computers as a host machine. The host machine is fed from a number of terminals and other external sources of information (see Fig 12 below).

The VDU screens can be located at overseas treasuries as well as at the central treasury. In this way overall treasury positions can be dealt with by the one system.

Some users have ETS for part of their treasury system. British Telecom

Fig 12

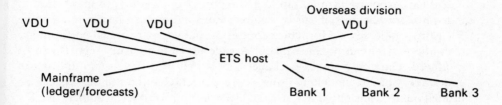

treasury use it for record keeping and reporting, with an interface with account balance reporting systems from various banks. Similarly Grand Metropolitan use ETS for record-keeping, with various balance reporting systems, a spreadsheet for decision support and a further bank electronic funds transfer system.

The ETS system costs upwards from £20,000, depending on the amount of customisation the customer requires.

Corporate treasury workstations – a brief review

There are a number of systems other than ETS marketed by banks and software houses. The bank systems are often made up of program parts purchased from software houses. This enables banks to produce their system more quickly than if they had written them themselves from scratch. Even so, some of the banks did write their own systems and are reputed to have spent large sums of money in doing so. It is debatable whether they have received a good return on this investment from sales so far.

There follows a brief description of a number of the systems on offer.

ABN BANK, CASHPRO.   This is a system designed to run on IBM compatible microcomputers, as are most of the other systems listed below, but in this case a hard disk is required. The FX module is only planned at present.

AMRO BANK, TREASURY MANAGER.   This is a modest system with spreadsheet interface, interest calculation and contract administration.

BANKERS TRUST, RESOURCE.   This more advanced package is written by ADS Associates, which is partly owned by Bankers Trust. It has an FX module planned and can already interface with accounting packages.

BANK OF AMERICA, MICROSTAR.   Microstar is the range of packages written by the bank's Swallow subsidiary whose systems have been successful in selling in the UK. The International Treasurer package in this range monitors FX and money market positions.

It tracks exposure through up to 300 reports from a total group position to individual transactions, if this is required. Revaluations can be run to compute FX gains and losses. Performance appraisals that compare actual performance with alternatives can be undertaken. A wide range of treasury reports can be produced. Data from other packages can be fed into the system and it can undertake 'what if' modelling using a spreadsheet. Confirmation letters can be printed out or transmitted to a telex or electronic mail service. Comparative FX quotes can be stored to build up a table for assessing banks performance on quoting. Calculations such as proxy swaps, net present value and discount to yield can be undertaken. The banking calendar can be input so that bank holidays are adjusted for. A file of bank information can be produced to track such things as contacts and facilities. In all, the package can record 32 currencies, 300 entities, 300 banks and some 7,000 transactions.

A further package, Communications Manager, can be used to automatically dial for bank balances to input to International Treasurer. Another package in the range, Report Generator, enables users to quickly produce new reports and output to all kinds of spreadsheets and other programs.

BARCLAYS BANK, BARCAM FOREX TRANSACTION MANAGER.   This is one of a series of Barclays Bank packages for the corporate treasurer. It is an easy to use menu driven system which can be set up and learned quickly: some two to three hours for set up of say 300 transactions in ten currencies. Operations are based on six basic functions. These are set up and maintenance, operation, revaluation, reports, end of day and year-end. Operation can be simplified so that one instruction set can produce confirmation letters, audit and management reports and a closing revaluation. It produces exposure statements in a number of formats: entry date, currency, account or maturity. Year-end audit trails and reports can also be produced. The transaction listing by date entry, for example, prints all transactions between any dates specified under the following headings:

1 transaction number;

2 date entered;

3 maturity date;

4 account name;

5 currency bought;

6 amount bought;

7 currency sold;

8 amount sold;

9 transaction rate;

10 equivalent local currency;

11 classification code; and

12 a short description.

BARCLAYS BANK, BARCAM TREASURY MASTER. This is a general corporate treasury package with extensive FX features. It can record and manage spot, forward, option forwards, options, tender to contract cover and swaps. Confirmation letters, accounting entries and exposure reports are produced. FX rates can be fed in directly from Reuters. It is possible to set tolerance levels for currencies to sound a warning of significant movements or to highlight input errors and the system can be used to calculate forward margin interest differentials together with broken date forwards. The integration of the system should help in savings of manual effort of input.

CHASE MANHATTAN BANK, GLOBAL MICROSTATION. This is a sophisticated package which can even produce confirmation letters, run different types of limits, interface with spreadsheets and produce a full range of reports. The FX module is called FX Contract Manager.

CHEMICAL BANK, CHEMLINK II. ChemLink II is mainly a cash management package but does have what if capabilities.

CITIBANK, SERPRIZE. A cash and exposure management system with lead and lag analysis options.

CREDIT SUISSE, TREASURER PC. This is a general treasury package that includes FX position reporting.

F INTERNATIONAL, TREASURY MANAGEMENT SYSTEM. TMS is a modular system with two FX subsystems plus money market and forecasting. A full range of reports, confirmation letters and outputs to an accounting system are produced.

FIRST CHICAGO BANK, FOREX MANAGER. This is part of the International First Manager package. Again confirmation letters, accounting interfaces and audit trails are produced. Modelling capabilities allow optimum hedge, changes in FX exposure level and FX rate movement simulation.

HONG KONG BANK, HEXAGON. Hexagon, is an integrated system to cover a wide range of a customer's dealings with the Hongkong bank, but normally not with other banks. A customer can view his FX contracts and maturities and even undertake small FX deals, at a rate quoted on the system, using his terminal.

HEWLETT PACKARD, HPCASH.   HPCASH is a minicomputer based treasury system that includes an FX module. The system can take FX spot and forward and options (American and European). Reports from the system are FX contracts, FX contracts pending, FX options, FX profits or losses by currency or purpose and FX exposure. There is an inbuilt interface with most of the main data exchange organisations to receive information from various banks. There are also accounting interfaces for both input and output.

INTEGRATED CASH MANAGEMENT SYSTEM.   This is from the software house of the same name, was originally designed for large treasuries, ran on a mainframe computer and cost in excess of US$100,000. There is now a version for IBM compatible microcomputers at a lesser cost. It is made up of eight modules including Foreign Exchange Manager. The system was written for the USA and is well regarded by its users there.

MANUFACTURERS HANOVER TRUST, INTERPLEX.   Interplex has a wide range of modules including Exposure Management I and II, Optimum Hedge Strategy, Currency Contract Management, Information and Analytical Systems, FX Forecasting and a Technical Momentum Model.

The Exposure Management module permits the following functions.

File selection and merge allows different currency files to be compared or merged. Data from different time periods can be compared.

Up to five forecast FX rates can be entered for what if simulations. Gains and losses can be calculated based on changes in these rates.

A currency exposure report can be produced for each entity in the system.

After-tax exposure reports can be constructed in each currency for one or a consolidation of entities. Output can be in the form of a graph if required.

The cost of hedging the position in each currency can be calculated.

The currency hedge simulation allows the effect of different hedge types to be compared.

Current FX rates can be fed into the system by communications link with the Manufacturers Hanover mainframe computer.

Most of the information contained in the module can be printed out.

The Exposure Management II incorporates amongst other things an exposure ageing printout for headoffice or divisions.

The Optimum Hedging module looks at correlated currencies on the basis of historic data. The model used is based on the fact that some currencies move in unison against each other with varying degrees of elasticity. The module measures correlations and elasticities continually from a daily updated FX database and combines the information with the user's FX position information to arrive at an optimal set of hedges that yield the lowest protection cost.

The module identifies positions that tend to offset each other or that increase risk due to past correlations. For instance, the Deutsche Mark and Dutch guilder will often move in close harmony, but say technical conditions in Holland might dictate a temporary change and a long position in one of the currencies could not be assumed to be a net with a short position in the other.

The module generates a report recommending complete or partial hedges that will leave the remaining exposures as an effective neutral position. The least cost hedging position is also produced.

The Currency Contract Management module is a fully integrated system for monitoring and accounting for spot and forward FX. The module holds all relevant information on each contract and automatically produces confirmation slips and payment instructions. Other features include:

1 details of FX facilities used and available with banks;

2 reports that can comply with accounting requirements such as amortised forward premiums and discounts;

3 cross references for matching FX contracts so that off-sets can be applied;

4 automatic, or manual, loading of spot and forward rates for 39 currencies updated three times daily;

5 simulations using currency forecasts;

6 simulations using dummy or proforma deals;

7 a wide variety of graphical presentations;

8 interfaces with other modules and packages such as spreadsheets; and

9 a calendar system to compute the days between contract dates.

The Information and Analytical module is a daily updated historic database. The User can select the historic information he requires from the following:

1 international economic and financial data for 75 countries;

2 spot and forward FX rates for 37 currencies; and

3 further economic and financial information relevant to international treasury from news services and over 60 publications.

The FX Forecasting module produces numerical forecasts of key variables such as gross national product, inflation, interest and FX rates. It does this by analysis of economic cycles, fundamentals and indicators. Input is updated once a month.

The final module is a Technical Momentum Model. It is strictly two models, a

30-day FX model which is frequently updated and a 30/90-day model with less frequent updates. The trading recommendations of the system cover five major currencies. The currency charts with construction lines can be seen. Testing over a four-year period indicated a 60–70% accuracy level with one model, rising to 70–80% when the two models were used jointly. A number of the Interplex modules can be used separately and some user's run them in conjuction with treasury modules from other suppliers. Courtaulds uses Interplex to collect FX rate information from the NatWest Rate Service but uses Bank of America modules for investment management.

MANUFACTURERS HANOVER TRUST, FOREIGN EXCHANGE SYSTEM.   This is a specialist FX system with a full range of exposure reports, FX contract listings and valuation reports. Current FX rates can be fed in and there is an eighteen year historical database of rates. Full accounts can be produced together with exposure management modelling and optimisation of hedging.

PRIVATBANKEN (Copenhagen).   This bank has a balance reporting package jointly developed with LR Systems that contains a currency risk simulator.

Not all corporate treasuries rely on package treasury systems. This may be because they have unusual needs, or have not found that the packages on offer deliver what they say they will, or again do not fit well with other packages. Treasuries that have written their own systems have done so on spreadsheets or database management systems. Even some of the bank systems are written in this type of program. The Barclays Bank FX Transaction Manager is written in dBase II, a database management system by Ashton Tate. Many of the bank systems also interface with either spreadsheet or database management systems.

The small volumes of transactions through most corporate treasuries mean that spreadsheets and database management systems can easily cope. Such systems are quick to develop and can easily be changed for changed circumstances. This possibility of change is important with the constant appearance of new treasury instruments. Most new instruments are an extension or collection of old instruments, but they still have at least slightly different processing needs. With a closed purchased system small changes can be as much of a problem as large ones, as both can require a new or changed module from the vendor software house. A reason why it is important to ensure that a purchased system will remain available and updated in the planned future operating period of your system.

Large-scale dealing systems

The large dealing systems are mainly used by banks and financial institutions, but will become of increasing interest to corporate treasuries as those treasuries increase their dealing expertise and size.

The systems are divided into three main functions; information supply and distribution, pre-transaction analysis and calculation and a record of the transaction. Most of the recent development work has been in information supply and distribution. These switching systems can accommodate a wide range of internal and external sources, and deliver them to each dealer's desk. Digital, rather than video, technology means that real time data from various sources can be consolidated, manipulated, graphed and used in models.

A diagram of a typical system is shown in Fig 13 below.

As a further illustration of what systems can do, there follows a brief description of various systems currently available.

ABACUS. This is a Reuter product that automatically calculates cross rates, broken dates and arbitrage opportunities. It is available on a Reuter terminal and uses up to the minute information from the main Reuters information services.

ADVANCED REUTER TERMINAL. Another system from Reuters, this is microcomputer based to allow manipulation of the Reuter pages. Split screen presentation of various pages and graphical presentation of the information is possible. An unusual feature is the capacity to search incoming news information for key words set by the user. If a report contains the keyword, an alert is sounded on the terminal to attract the user's attention.

BANKMASTER DECISION SUPPORT TOOL KIT. This is part of the BankMaster system, from Banking Decision Systems, which offers asset and liability management, budgeting, profit planning, strategic planning and management reporting. The system can be run on a mainframe, a micro or via a timesharing bureau. The Decision Support Tool Kit is of relevance to the dealing operation. It offers modelling, spreadsheet functions, what if, multimodel linking, a custom report writer language and graphics capabilities.

DEALER'S CHOICE. This system is from International Banking Systems and is a dealing and decision support system with direct transaction input by the dealer using touch sensitive screens. Functions and input are quickly and easily achieved using the touch screen. The system takes all the main information services in digital form to allow manipulation as required. Internal information sources and feeds to the backoffice are also accommodated. A full range of management,valuation and profitability reports are available. Dealing positions are microcomputers on a local area network. It is therefore easy to change the number and siting of dealing positions.

DORIS. This is an IP Sharp Associates two-way information system for rates and transactions. It is often used by bank dealing rooms to service provincial dealing operations. FX rates are passed out from the main dealing room to the

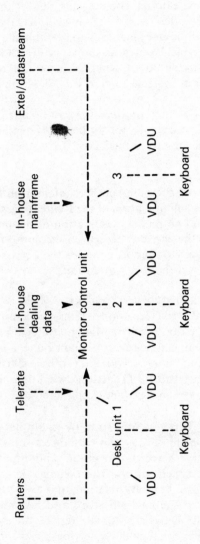

Fig 13

branches. Transactions undertaken by the branches are communicated back to the main dealing room to update the overall position of the bank.

EXPOSURE MANAGEMENT SYSTEM. Devon, after Devon AG the supplier of the system, is the commonly used name for this system for trading and recording futures, options and normal FX spot and forward. For the dealer there are various simulation and calculation features, but for the backoffice there is a good deal of support. There are confirmations, brokerage and margin calculations, payment instructions and spreadsheet and ledger package interfaces.

FIDESSA. This system from Intercom Data Systems is an information collection, representation and distribution system. It has three elements; a message router to handle incoming information, an automatic editor to manage processing and a distributor to send to the result. Output can be digital or video.

FOREXTREND. Forexia is a currency forecasting company which publishes currency forecasts on Prestel. Forextrend is the technical analysis software package that it sells for customers who want to do their own forecasting. A wide range of currencies are dealt with. It presents its analysis with line graphs, point and figure charts, relative strength charts and histograms.

FOXI. This is a predeal information and decision support system marketed by Software Sciences. The system receives feeds from the external services and can supply information back to them. Calculations which the system can undertake include arbitrage possibilities, forward rates, cross rates, basket rates and yields. An interface with IBM systems allows some access to internal data bases. There is a version for small dealing rooms called MINIFOXI.

GDRSS. Global Dealing Room Support System is a transaction record and management system for dealers marketed by Intelcom Data Systems. Consolidated information is produced and reported as positions, liquidity, transactions done and credit utilisation. External information systems, such as Reuters, can be fed into the system and it will also undertake calculation and modelling. Output for backoffice systems, management reports and profitability reports can be obtained.

GLCS. This is a position keeper and global limits system from IP Sharp Associates. IP Sharp has an international communications network which is used by the system to aggregate the worldwide dealings of multinational customers. The normal information consolidated is client exposures, currency positions, limits, deals, cashflows and liquidity.

GLOBAL LIMITS. This is the GEISCO version of GLCS described above. In this case the GEISCO international communications network is used.

HEDDS. This product from Helix Software Consultants, is a deal record and position system. The system provides dealers with positions, exposures, account details and maturity profiles. For the backoffice, confirmations, payment instructions, journal entries and adhoc reports can be produced. Multi-level passwords are used to secure the system.

HSBS. The High Speed Broadcast System from CAP Group is an information processor which distributes centrally captured external and internal information to dealing positions. Data can be retransmitted to external customers, say, through Reuters, after processing.

IBOS. This is the CAP group transaction entry and position keeper for the medium-sized dealing room. There are calculation routines and what if modelling is available. Transaction entry is by keyboard or touch sensitive screen by the dealer or a position clerk. The system displays the present currency position and the unutilised credit line of the customer at the time of input, so that it is immediately clear if controls are exceeded. Once a deal is accepted into the system, positions and limits are updated for all users. Security is by multi-level passwords. A range of management reports produced include valuations, correspondent bank balance projections, interest differential analysis, brokerage payments and gains and losses on dealings.

IDEAL. This is the Image Software system which combines integration of internal and external information sources with position keeping, calculation, modelling, correspondent bank balances and output to the books of account.

IDF. The Integrated Data Feed system from Aregon International, uses digital processing and feeds to dealing positions. Calculation facilities are being included with the package and enhancement to a full dealing system is being investigated.

IDS. Datacorp's IDS is an information processor from external and internal sources to supply multiple dealing positions. A subroutine called Analyser monitors the usage of the different information sources to assess their cost-effectiveness. Support packages such as calculators, graphics, statistics and analysis can be added to IDS.

I.D.S. The Forex Advisory Services I.D.S. system is a realtime system offering position keeping, limits, liquidity management, calculation and modelling.

MIDAS DRS. This is the dealing system part of the widely used MIDAS package from BIS Software. It integrates external data services, calculation, modelling and position keeping. The calculation and modelling system will find cashflow gaps, calculate the cost of closing a position at a given rate, monitor the profit or loss on FX positions and monitor liquidity and limits. The system fully integrates with the MIDAS IBS backoffice to give correspondent bank balances, payment instructions, accounting entries and full management reports.

MONEY GRAPHICS SERVICE. This is a historical analysis of trends and prices from Reuters. A graphical presentation can be given of the movements of any of the main currencies over a period of one day to one year.

ODIN. Alimand Computer System has the dealing system ODIN which provides information, calculation, modelling and position taking. Up to 64 dealing positions can be supported. Automatic generation of dealing tickets and a direct feed to the internal accounting system, can also improve contacts with the backoffice.

There are various dealing features. Trial deal allows a dealer to check the feasibility of prospective deals with regard to various limits set in the system. There is a deal reminder feature to refer back to previous simulations. These old deals can be resubmitted to see if they work with new parameters. Actual deals can be input in the FX deal module to monitor any excesses of dealing limits, to check positions or average rates and to feed to the backoffice. Input of actual deals can be either singly as outright deals or as swap deals. The swap facility avoids duplication of input effort. If an entry exceeds the dealing limits in the system, that entry is not accepted until a password override is used. Once an entry is accepted, the whole range of positions, limits and accounts are updated.

The FX position module gives a comprehensive analysis of FX positions in all currencies for any required period. An overview position screen shows the overall position for each currency. Two further screens position detail by currency and position detail by period. There is also a facility to focus on a specific period and to produce further detail down to constituent days. Positions can be given in the actual currency and in a base currency, say US dollars.

An internal deal module allows a splitting of profits and losses on dealing for different dealing desks or departments. These deals are put through the main system in the same way as actual FX deals.

OPPORTUNITY. This is an advanced calculation system from Helix Software Consultants. Split-screen options allow various calculations to be undertaken at once. Over 20 main functions can be operated with a minimum of key strokes. The system is split into a Supervisor module that undertakes start of day and update tasks, and Calculator. It is Calculator that computes currency baskets, spot, forward, arbitrage and various moneymarket calculations. The system can be directly fed from Reuters with FX and moneymarket figures on which to base the calculations.

OPTION PRICE CALCULATOR. The name of this Tullett and Tokyo system gives a good indication of what it does. It obtains its FX and other rates by data phone link from the Futrend database in London. The system calculates such things as fair prices of options, implied volatilities and sensitivities to change.

PC-BANK.   CBS Banking Software has a backoffice system for departments of large banks down to small banks. There is a separate FX module but it is run in conjunction with standing data and general ledger modules. Reporting and exposure modules also operate across all other modules. The exposure module sets up and monitors counterparty, group and country limits. It allows the normal gap, open position and limit excess reports. The FX module records deals and prepares confirmations, an FX dealing diary, correspondent bank projections and outstanding deals per customer.

REUTER DEALER PACKAGES (CALCULATION).   This system uses the existing Reuter keyboad to calculate arbitrage, cross rates, broken dates, futures arbitrage and hedging. It feeds from the Reuter information service.

REUTER DEALER PACKAGES (RCIS).   This is a Reuter package which can capture information from most sources and route it to dealing desks.

REUTER MONEY DEALING SERVICE.   This system allows a dealer to transact actual deals over the Reuter Monitor terminal.

RPKS.   This is Reuter's position keeping service. The dealer inputs by a small number of movements on an electronic tablet. This updates his position and that for the whole dealing room. The package can be integrated with other dealing systems.

SPOT.   This Cortex Computer Systems package provides dealing room and backoffice administration. External information service feeds can be used, data entry by dealers can be checked by the backoffice and confirmation instructions can be produced. A wide range of reports can be generated. Restrictions on who can use particular parts of the package can be applied.

STREAM.   This is another global control product from IP Sharp Associates, but this time in association with SWIFT. Communications are either by the SWIFT network or IP Sharp network so that the cheapest method can be used. Worldwide risk figures can be quickly produced.

TANTUS.   This a position keeping system from Data Logic with input via an electronic pad or touch sensitive screen. Information from external and internal sources can be routed to dealing desks and an advanced dealing support and backoffice interface addition is under development.

TELETRAC. Telerate has this microcomputer-based system which feeds from their information system to produce calculation, analysis and graphics. There is also a dial-up facility to allow access to various information sources.

TELETRADE BUSINESS SYSTEM. British Telecom are the suppliers of this communications system. It is a touch controlled VDU screen that combines telephone and telex switching and computer data retrieval. Information can be changed by means of a keyboard and stored or transmitted even when the system is being used to make a telephone call.

TRADE. This is the Control Data Financial Information Services information switching system. A dealer can combine data from different sources (internal and external), create composite pages and graphics, perform calculations and undertake market analysis.

TRADE EVALUATOR. The name here indicates what the package does. Money brokers Tullett and Tokyo lease the microcomputer software that feeds from their Futrend database by data phone link. A dealer can set up a trading strategy or rule on the system and test it against past and possible future rates. He can refine his strategy in the light of the results and finally carry out and monitor the strategy.

TRADER ONE. This is the data entry and exposure management system from Control Data Financial Information Services. Input by a touch sensitive tablet gives realtime exposure entry, single transaction entry and dealing ticket production. The system will produce a range of management reports on positions, valuations and profits and losses, together with direct output to an accounting system.

VALUTA. This system from Informatik Forum combines information provision and management with facilities for data manipulation and calculation. Internal and external data bases can be captured, reconfigured and retransmitted say to Reuters or Telerate. FX calculation subroutines include swaps, cross rates, EMS and broken dates.

FX rate services

Many of the dealing packages use what has been described as external services to obtain FX rates. This section deals with those services available in the UK for use by the treasuries of banks and corporations.

CEEFAX BBC CITYNEWS TELETEX. 18 currencies, the sterling FX index, comments relevant to FX rates and some interest rates. Opening, mid-day and closing rates are given for four of the currencies. Economic information is given on BBC Moneyfile. The only running cost in the UK is the cost of a standard television licence.

CITYCALL. Sterling and US dollar rates against 16 major currencies from National Westminster Bank are given. The service is provided by British Telecom in spoken form at a modest cost per minute with a half-price cost outside business hours, when only the previous close is given. This is one of the few examples of a spoken information service.

DATASTREAM. Datastream International offer a wide range of databases that includes 128 FX rates and currency futures and options.

ESM FINANCIAL MANAGEMENT SYSTEM. This system from Electron Systems (Marketing) takes information encoded in a television signal and allows it to be displayed on a microcomputer and input into other systems if required. The information is that available with a teletext television plus other pages from Midland Bank. Current FX rates are available for 15 major currencies, spot and forward updated every five minutes. A general commentary is available together with graphics, calculation facilities and what if modelling.

ESPRIT. An Extel service which continuously feeds raw FX and other data for a user's system to format.

EXAMINER. Another Extel service with FX and moneymarket updated only hourly.

FT CITYLINE. Telephone message of FX spot rates updated hourly.

GLOBAL REPORT MONEY SERVICE. This is the Citibank service quoting spot and forward rates for 55 currencies and commentary, recommendations and consensus forecasts. Eight other banks in addition to Citibank, plus other information services, provide the rates.

INFOSERVICE. This service from IP Sharp gives the previous day's closing spot FX rate for 14 currencies and forwards for five currencies. Graphics and package interfaces are available.

INTERPLEX. From MH Financial Mangement (Manufacturers Hanover), this database has current and historic information on 75 currencies and is updated three times a day.

MARKET RATE SERVICES. This is the Chase Manhattan Bank system reporting FX rates on 25 currencies. It is updated several times a day.

MARS MARKETS.   This service with various FX spot and forward quotes, is only available to users of the Morgan Guaranty Trust cash management system.

NATWEST NETWORK TREASURY DATA SERVICE.   This National Westminster Bank service gives spot and forward rates on 24 currencies. The service does have calculation capabilities and is updated three times a day.

ORACLE, TELETEX.   Barclays Bank supply FX spot and some forward rates on 28 currencies to ITV Channel 4 for continuous broadcast in the television signal. Updates are every two minutes. The only running cost of using this service is the standard television licence fee.

PRESTEL, CITISERVICE.   This service from ICV Information Systems offers spot rates for 36 currencies and forwards for 15, all against sterling and US dollars. Rates are supplied by various banks and brokers with a continuous update between 7.30am and 5pm. Information can be supplied to a monitor, television or a microcomputer.

QUOTRON.   There are various financial services on offer from Quotron Systems. FX rates are taken from Telerate under the name Cash Market Profile.

REUTER INTERNATIONAL MONEY RATES.   The Monitor service giving around 100 currencies is the best known of the FX information services. There are some 60,000 terminals around the world.

REUTER MONITOR MONEY MANAGER SERVICE.   This is the Reuters service for small to medium-sized corporate treasuries. It gives access to some of the FX and money market quotes from the full Reuters services.

REUTER POCKETWATCH.   This is a radio receiver the size of a small calculator, that gives FX and deposit rates for the major currencies. Transmissions can be received within 25 miles of London.

TELERATE FINANCIAL INFORMATION SYSTEM.   The full Telerate system has some 20,000 pages of information including all types of FX. There are some 42,000 screens in use worldwide.

TELERATE UK DOMESTIC SERVICE.   This is a service introduced in 1987 for corporate treasuries who do not want the full Telerate service. Access is limited to 200 pages of FX, money market, gilts, options, futures, indices, equities, metals, economic indicators and news.

Ledger packages

There are a number of banking ledger packages, some of which have been mentioned in connection with the compatible dealing systems. Most are very large and expensive with therefore little application outside the banking area.

For the corporate treasury there are some more modest accounting packages and also some of the corporate treasury workstations previously described, have ledger packages.

An example of an accounting package is in the Thorn EMI Computer Software SMB-Plus range. Multicurrency ledgers work on a base currency. Revaluations between this base currency and the actual currency can be undertaken and differences automatically posted to a separate exchange differences account. A full FX exposure report can also be printed.

Shortlands Gold is another suite of programs with a multicurrency facility. Subsidiary ledgers can be held in any currency and a consolidation to a reporting currency produced. The system can be run on a microcomputer.

Choosing a system

For all the types of system that have been dealt with in this chapter, there are points that should be considered when selecting a system for a particular application. They can be broken down into the following considerations.

Design considerations, such as whether the system can be extended for foreseeable and unforeseeable future needs. Will the software house vendor, or acting for the vendor, update the package for changes in the general operating conditions, such as statutory changes? Does the system easily interface with other systems which are likely to be used?

Dealing aids, such as immediate update of all reported positions for transacted deals. It is possible to assess accurately the results of deals and the reasons for these results?

Control considerations, such as verification of input and the isolation of mistakes. Quick notification of the exposures produced by deals, in case some had not been forseen. Checks and controls to minimise the risk of fraud.

Reporting and accounting elements, such as management reports that show all important exposures and profiles to aid management decisions. The system must properly recognise value days for record purposes and dealing dates (ie spot FX is dealt two business days before the value date). The system should have full accounting capabilities or should be able to interface with a system that does have such capabilities. A range of statistical reports as to deal volumes and counterparties is also useful to assess relative efficiencies in relationships.

Such checklists are very useful, but still an important criteria in selecting the best package is to see how well it fits into the environment in which it will operate. Another point is the user's expectation and skill. One user will want an automatic system, whilst a further user may prefer detailed steps so that he can pick an optimum path through the program. Our first user may require a set of features that bear little resemblence to the wants of another user. Finally the cost that one user will consider acceptable may not be so for other users.

These points illustrate that it is almost impossible to endorse one system as the best for all users requiring that type of system. This past chapter has given brief notes on a large number of systems and it is hoped that it may be of some benefit to readers. The user has to decide on his minimum requirements and then start the search. The section 'Specifying a Computerised FX Management System' below deals further with what is required of many kinds of computerised FX management systems.

SPECIFYING A COMPUTERISED FX MANAGEMENT SYSTEM

SUMMARY

This chapter deals in general terms with what is required of a computerised FX management system, whether bespoke or a standard package.

What is needed

The corporate treasurer is bombarded with offers of help from banks and software houses. Most contend that theirs is the 'complete' system, with all the treasurer's needs. Closer examination usually reveals a good coverage in one, or a number of aspects of FX management, but nothing like the complete coverage offered. To be fair to the suppliers, different treasurers will have special needs and a complete off-the-shelf package may well be impossible.

The major shortcoming of the offered systems is the limitation on the sources of data. Any one system will only use part of available market rates, bank balances and internal corporate figures. A full Reuters or Telerate service will normally supply all the necessary market rates and is generally taken as an expensive stand-alone service. A cheaper but almost as good service would be needed to augment the ideal comprehensive package.

The spread of accessable bank accounts is the key factor. In October 1984, Alan Clements the ICI finance director, said 'a different set of equipment for each bank is not an acceptable long-term solution'. The principle remains the same.

An emerging compromise is the use of the same hardware with differing access packages. IBM compatibility is the widely accepted standard for hardware, as this is already in the possession of most treasurers. The next step is to make the software very similar in operation. Operations staff do not like to have to learn a number of totally different operating methods, which can become confused.

The best method will always be one system which can access all necessary data sources. Systems should allow an element of access customisation. There are big efficiency benefits to the treasurer in widening his access range, so that it will be worth some effort on his part to achieve this. Suppliers should not think that simplicity regarding access methods is necessarily the most important factor.

The favoured present area of expansion for treasury packages is the decision support area. This is an area where the needs of each treasurer as perceived by him, will vary greatly. Therefore this is an area where systems designers should proceed warily, For example, there is a wide range of views as to which measure of foreign currency exposure is to be managed and how the calculation of foreign currency exposed is made. There is a strong argument for packages which allow the individual treasurer easily to superimpose his own decision framework on a broadly defined standard package. Whether the FX system is a standard package, a customised package, or a specially written system, there are various considerations to apply.

Total system considerations

How will the treasurer assess a system?

1 His objectives

In a range from essential to preferred.

2 Fit with his business

Often a comparison with the present manual system if it has been successful. What new disciplines will the system impose?

3 Ease of cross section comparison

Can incomplete deals be accurately shown and valued?

4 Is system output acceptable?

Report format and detail considerations.

5 Is the whole system sufficiently furthering the business?

6 What are the implementation problems?

Evaluation of the financial considerations

What are the cost considerations which a treasurer will apply?

1 Initial cost considerations

What are the total costs of the system, including all hidden costs?

2 The treasurer's special requirements

How easy is it to put through essential modifications? Can amended requirements be actioned cheaply and quickly?

3 Costs of new stationery

Probably one of the smaller costs of the new system.

4 New communication link costs

Tied lines can be very expensive depending on distance. Even dial-up line costs can be substantial for some systems.

5 Conversion costs

The cost of setting up any required data base and parallel running costs, are examples of such costs.

6 Running costs

Materials necessary for output and storage.
Effort and materials required for adequate back-up in case of systems failure.
Staff with new capabilities for the new system.
Insurance cover for the physical equipment and the damage that might ensue from its misuse.

Any vendor of standardised products will have difficulty with the discerning customer. Corporate treasurers tend to be more sophisticated (or do I mean awkward?) and discerning than many. However, having a specially written system can be spectacularly expensive and time-consuming. Any treasurer has to consider long and hard before rejecting standard packages as the solution to his systems problems. Does he really need all those personalised features? Can they be justified on a cost basis?

TREASURY TRAINING AND STRUCTURES

SUMMARY

This chapter deals with the staffing background of a treasury department.

Management training

Study of the treasury discipline, as a separate finance area, is relatively recent but has, even so, reached a high degree of sophistication. Most large concerns now tend to prefer to have a treasury specialist as their treasurer, rather than a finance generalist. Research conducted in the UK by the London Business School has shown that treasury operations within UK companies tend to be less sophisticated than those in their European counterparts. The fact that 70% of UK treasurers are accountants, not specifically trained for treasury, may have some bearing on this (Ascher and Kind, 1985).

In the UK this has given rise to the formation of an Association of Corporate Treasurers to indicate a degree standard of technical proficiency in members. In addition, numerous commercial organisations offer short courses on treasury matters (not all of them solely notable for the quality of their lunches).

Many treasury operations have recruited staff from bank FX dealing rooms. These are large companies such as BP, Volvo and Elf-Acquitaine, but smaller companies have also done the same.

Managers must ensure that they are not wedded to some out-of-date doctrine. Keynes pointed out that the most practical of men, who believe themselves to be quite exempt from any intellectual influences, are actually slaves of some defunct economist (Keynes, 1936). The foreign exchange market is one of those situations where the volume of information, the lack of structure in the task (arguable?) and the uncertainty of the environment, defy planning and programming. In such situations the intuitive manager's style can be highly effective (McKenney and Keen, 1980). The good decision is often 90% information and 10% inspiration (Davis, 1979).

Treasury management of multinational companies has no excuse to be ignorant of the technical tools available and effective. They have a duty to deal in the FX market in a professional manner (Bailey, 1985). Most avail themselves of these opportunities and prepare their staffs reasonably. Today's successful manager works to old-fashioned principles by using contemporary tools and techniques.

Flexibility

The need for flexibility here is the need for instant reaction to significant happenings in the FX market. An international treasury department must not be caught unawares by changes in currencies in which it has a financial interest. Structures and operating procedures must be such that valuable time is not lost. Sufficient dealing authority must be available quickly, or serious exchange losses could be suffered whilst such authority is obtained. There is a delicate balance required between controls to protect against fraud and overtrading and speed of action to obviate exchange losses. Most treasury dealing systems give foreign exchange dealers a fair degree of latitude in their dealings because of the significant possibility of exchange loss with a system of strong controls. A system of dealing limits, as discussed earlier in the book, is a good flexible control method.

Structure

A treasury operation must have a well thought out structure. The considerations relating to prospective operations must be:

1 volume of transactions;
2 complexity of input from other departments; and
3 complexity of instruments to be dealt in.

With the answers to these questions, the level of support both human and machine can be assessed. The volume of work produced by the above factors will impose immediate minimum requirements on staff. Treasury is one area where fast turn-around of work is essential. It is surprising how small many treasury staffs are. Multinational companies with vast accounting departments, may have a treasurer, an assistant and a few dealing and backoffice staff. This is probably a tribute to good organisation and resistance to being saddled with large, number crunching, duties. It is important to insist on refined and accurate information from supplying departments.

To define a structure, it will be necessary to assume a large FX operation. For a small treasury the functions will be undertaken by more than one person. The large structure will have a treasurer and a number of assistant treasurers.

Below this will be the dealers or treasury assistants. The title that is used would tend to depend on the type of operation. If it is unusual for FX positions to be traded and dealing room staff purely function by laying off risk to the banks, the dealing room staff are normally called treasury assistants. However, if FX positions are actively traded, the dealing room is more likely to have dealers.

The dealing room

A large dealing room will be controlled by a chief dealer, who may not actually deal himself. He is responsible for the budget for the dealing room and to see that management policy is clear to all dealers. Informing senior management of any important news or disquiet in the dealing room is also his job. He may well lead the discussion in the early morning meeting in the dealing room before dealing begins. This meeting is an important forum for discussion of forecasts and strategies for the day. The chief dealer is also responsible for training by holding internal classes or arranging for external classes. He also has to assess the effectiveness of individual dealers and advise and caution when a person's standard is slipping.

Below the chief dealer are senior dealers responsible for groups of currencies or one major currency. They implement and develop strategies, under the guidance of the chief dealer. They also supervise a number of more junior dealers, monitor their positions and deal with any difficult problems that arise. They are often assisted by the more junior dealers when their major currency is being very actively dealt.

Responsible to the senior dealers are FX dealers helped by junior dealers. FX dealers will be in charge of less active currencies, whilst junior dealers, trainees and position clerks will provide support by keeping positions up to date, input into the computer dealing system, update information screens, man communications links and keep contact with the backoffice.

There will tend to be a subdivision between dealers looking after the spot position and those dealing in the forward market. The training and skill required for the two markets is different, but few non-banks can afford the staffing levels of separate dealers for spot and forward in each currency. Most corporate dealing rooms will have the same dealer trading spot and forward in a currency.

It may be difficult to define what makes a good dealer. He certainly has to be a survivor, good at understanding the changing nature of markets and quick to react to new opportunities and situations. He has to be able to work under stress, be willing to accept responsibility, be able to make quick decisions in reversing a previous stance. There has to be an atmosphere of trust and reliability in a dealing room. Very large sums can change hands in a very short time. Any distrust or hesitation can seriously impede the performance of the team.

A dealer also has to be trusted in the FX market. He can very quickly gain a reputation as a good or bad dealer. The FX market is one place where you need all the friends that you can get. Frank information and views of the market from other dealing rooms are very useful for a dealer to form his own opinion. Conversely, a disliked dealer will find it very difficult to get much help if he is in trouble with a deal.

The dealer needs to develop an instinctive feel for the FX market. He has to overcome the natural tendency to try to salvage something from a loss making situation. He has to feel what the market will do next, not stick with his own view while the market goes in the other direction. Added to this, a broad theoretical knowledge is very useful. It needs to be broad because so many different things can affect the FX market. Not just economic and financial learning but geography, history, psychology and politics.

At the end of the day it is a good combination of favourable factors which produce the successful dealer. It is the consistent performer rather than erratic returns which impress the boss and lead to reward.

The Backoffice

The backoffice is the collective name for the operational support team for the dealing room. It has to process the transactions undertaken in the dealing room, check for errors and input the information into the financial records of the business. As dealing rooms become more mechanised, the backoffice also has less paper to input. At one time slips describing every deal were passed back from the dealing room to be laboriously processed. It is now possible to have the dealer input the deal into a machine system. There is still the need for a backoffice function, but it can be much more streamlined with time to check every deal carefully before passing the entry through to the main financial system.

The major recent problem for backoffice operations has been the rapid growth of the new instruments. Dealing rooms are very keen to use the latest instruments, if only to assess their usefulness. The problems normally arise in the backoffice if processing is highly automated. Such automated systems are difficult to alter to take account of the new instruments. Either a short-term manual patch system has to be applied or the backoffice decrees that there should be no further dealings in the instruments. Neither alternative is ideal. If a number of manual sub-systems are built in over time, a very awkward and inefficient system can result. The alternative of banning all exotic instruments will create tension in contacts with the dealing room and dealing advantage may be lost.

The personnel structure of a large backoffice will be headed by a supervisor to co-ordinate the other staff. All other staff would tend to report to this supervisor. The responsibility areas would be broken down as follows:

1 checking and confirmations;

2 reconciliations;

3 total liabilities;

4 accounts input; and

5 filing and typing.

This structure ensures that once a deal has been checked on receipt from the dealing room, confirmations are sent out to further agree the position. The reconciliations section check the returning confirmations and other external information, such as correspondent bank nostro balances. Total liabilities area reviews the total position resulting from dealing and accounts input is responsible for the input into the books of account. The machine system advising the dealers of their positions may be fed from the backoffice, but with the urgent need for the information it is more likely to be fed by clerks or junior dealers in the dealing room.

The backoffice function is every bit as important as the dealing room although this is not always obvious. The backoffice has to scrutinise deals quickly, as errors in FX dealing can be costly and the cost can increase speedily with time. Information from the dealing room, the counter-party and various banks and clearing houses has to be reconciled with the minimum of delay.

CASE STUDY – GROUP FX MANAGEMENT

SUMMARY

This case study shows many of the points raised in other chapters of this book. Not every point can be illustrated as this would lead to excessive length and complexity. One good way of running a treasury is shown. Other methods may be just as good.

Conagtrac

The company Conagtrac is a fictitious multinational company which manufactures and distributes construction and agricultural tractors. Subsidiary companies manufacture and sell tractors in various European countries. Manufacturing is in France, Germany and the UK. There are selling operations in most of the large European countries. Some of these selling operations may only consist of a small office.

In recent years tractor sales have been declining. This is due to low farm incomes and reduced levels of construction work. The Conagtrac Group is in a financially weak situation and is suffering intense competition from Japan, the US and other European manufacturers. There is a strong argument for strict financial controls but the Group cannot afford to miss any financial opportunities that its competitors might grasp.

It has been decided to centralise group treasury operations in the UK headquarters. It is felt that this is the best way to exercise some control and also bring together the best treasury staff from around the Group. Conagtrac subsidiaries have in the past enjoyed a high level of autonomy, but there is a general acceptance that the subsidiaries have enough tractor market problems at present to swamp local management.

The decision to centralise the treasury creates a need for very good financial information flows from the subsidiaries. As the subsidiaries are already hard pressed, they cannot be expected to spend much time producing this information. There is great advantage in linking requirements with what is easily available from the subsidiary's accounting system.

Conagtrac companies have always sent a detailed monthly accounting package to head office. The first exercise is to see what necessary treasury information is already included in the package. As package information is loaded into the head office computer accounting system, it is easy to extract this information in any required format as a computer report.

There is some monthly information which cannot be found from the present forms. It is helpful if additional requests for figures are in a format similar to that of the existing forms. Thought should also be given to the way in which the subsidiary collects the information. Formats should ease collection. This improves accuracy and speed of completion. The treasury can easily reorder figures once they are stored in the computer.

The bulk of the information to be collected monthly will relate to estimates of the future FX exposure. A copy of one month's form is shown in the example at the end of this case study. Figures from one month need to be compared with those from previous returns. Big changes in the forecast for any one future month will need to be investigated. Over a period, an assessment of the accuracy of estimates can be gauged. The final forecasts produced rely on the value of the information input.

Conagtrac has spent some time reviewing the forms received and questioning subsidiaries when figures look wrong. Information is fed into a medium-sized mainframe computer which is used for various head office processing. It would be possible to use a large microcomputer to process the figures if the mainframe had not been available. The process run is included with the month end accounting processing to save administration costs. The treasury reports are printed with the accounts and distributed with them to the finance director for his information.

The treasurer receives two copies of the exposure forms and a consolidation of the exposure forms. He can always refer to the monthly accounts held in the nearby Accounts department if he wishes.

Treasury is staffed by two people, the treasurer himself and an assistant treasurer. The assistant treasurer undertakes clerical and analytical roles and would probably more accurately be described as a treasury assistant. The finance director takes most of the decisions in the department when the treasurer is absent. General position and dealing policy is decided by the finance director and the treasurer jointly. Every few months the treasurer organises a meeting of all the senior head office managers of departments that suffer from FX fluctuations (manufacturing, purchasing and marketing). The meeting starts with a talk from the treasurer on currency prospects for the near future and recent exposure figures from the subsidiaries. There is then a general discussion of these points and each manager is asked for any special considerations that have arisen or are about to arise in their departments.

The treasurer has a modest microcomputer-based technical analysis program to form a view on immediate FX rate movements. The various free bank commentaries and regular telephone calls to bank FX dealers supplement the analysis program. The treasurer will also discuss local currency prospects when he is in contact with subsidiary managers. To help subsidiary managers, the treasurer regularly telexes his own brief commentary on prospects for their currency.

As the group is in a weak financial position, there is concern that large currency losses should not be incurred. The treasurer monitors transactional, translational and economic FX exposure with the use of the monthly forms: the forms from the subsidiaries and one he produces of his own position. He does not want to cover completely all exposures because competitor companies may not be covered and could take advantage of an improving currency position whilst he would be locked in. To remain wholly uncovered would leave too much FX exposure for a weak group. Conagtrac has significant economic exposures to yen and US dollar-based manufacturing competitors. The group can, with a small time-lag, switch some production between sterling, French franc or Deutsche Mark bases. Luckily translation exposures are small in most currencies.

The treasurer decides to undertake a policy of selective hedging. This is a scheme of constant review of currency cross rates and forecasts. At times of uncertainty and high loss probability, positions are almost entirely covered. When there appears to be a good chance of a currency profit, the proportion covered is reduced.

The first tool of exposure management used by the treasurer is a currency netting system. He has purchased a microcomputer-based package to do the calculations and matrix printout. The system does not automatically produce confirmatory letters and telexes but he did not consider it worth paying more for a package with this facility. Subsidiaries notify him of their foreign currency receipts and payments monthly. Netting settlements are all made on 25th of each month and subsidiaries are asked to plan to make as many FX receipts and payments, through the clearing on that day, as they can. Subsidiaries send an initial telex of receipts and payments on the 20th of the month. The treasurer telexes back with any questions on inconsistences. He aims to have a clear position for dealing on the 23rd. After he has completed the spot FX deals for value the 25th, he notifies all the subsidiaries of their single receipt or payment in their own currency. Settlements are made through a number of clearing accounts (one for each currency) maintained by him. Weekends and other bank holidays vary the above dates in some months but otherwise there is strict discipline on keeping to dates so as not to hold up the system.

Apart from netting, the treasurer does not use many of the other forms of natural hedging. As for leading and lagging currency payments, he would normally want to pay at the last possible moment and therefore has little scope to lag. He would only pay early if the interest cost was less than any likely exchange loss or alternative hedge. What he does do is to encourage subsidiaries to borrow their local currency to limit exposure in that currency.

For further hedging he uses instruments purchased from banks. The ones he finds most appropriate are forwards and options. He considered buying exchange traded futures and options but found the standard sizes and periods and margin payment a nuisance. Tailored options from a bank will be more expensive, but he considers it worth it. He uses forwards when he considers that there is a good chance he will suffer an exchange loss if he remains uncovered. Options are more appropriate when there is period of uncertainty ahead. To keep the option premium cost down, he uses a strike price well below the current spot or forward at a point of significant loss. He therefore only protects himself against a large loss. He also considers writing an option which would limit his possible profit in exchange for a definite premium now to offset the premium he has paid.

Example of an FX exposure form

Part of the Conagtrac group is a US subsidiary. It is a selling and distribution company with some warehouse property to store tractors. The US subsidiary has taken out some forward contracts; short-term ones of US$40,000 and long-term ones of US$250,000. The balance sheet of the subsidiary is as follows:

	$ '000
Receivables	150
Other current assets	300
	450
Payables	(60)
Other current liabilities	(90)
	300
Fixed assets	300
	600
Share capital and opening reserves	500
Profit for the year	100
	600

These figures are used for the first 'This Month End' column in the forecast on p 116 below. A progressive forecast is used for the succeeding month ends.

It is clear that the different measures of exposure show different change factors although with a broadly similar trend. Management has to decide which of the measures it intends to concentrate on.

CURRENCY EXPOSURE FORECAST

CONAGTRAC

US SUBSIDIARY

CURRENCY... US $'000

DATE..

Future months—estimated

	This mth end	Mth 1	Mth 2	Mth 3	Mth 4	Mth 5	Mth 6
Cash flows							
Receivables	150	150	140	150	160	140	130
Cash hedges (short forwards)	(40)	(20)	(10)				
Payables	(60)	(50)	(50)	(60)	(70)	(60)	(60)
1 Cash flow exposure	50	80	80	90	90	80	70
Balance sheet/current assets	300	300	310	310	310	320	310
Less current liabilities	(90)	(100)	(90)	(90)	(80)		
Fixed assets	300	300	300	300	300	300	300
Foreign exchange contracts (Long)	(250)	(250)	(200)	(200)	(150)	(100)	(100)
2 Net asset/liability accounting exposure	310	330	400	410	470	600	580
Less opening net equity position in currency	(500)	(500)	(500)	(500)	(500)	(500)	(500)
3 Profit and loss exposure	(190)	(170)	(100)	(90)	(30)	100	80
4 Economic influences not quantified in the accounts	Yen based competitor						

WORLD CURRENCIES LIST

SUMMARY

This chapter lists countries with separate currencies, notes the name given to their currency and gives the SWIFT identification code, based on international standard ISO 4217. The SWIFT codes are gaining acceptance as a common standard for describing currencies. In some countries other currencies may also be accepted for domestic payments.

Currency units of the world

Country	Currency	SWIFT code
Afghanistan	Afgani	AFA
Albania	Lek	ALL
Algeria	Dinar	DZD
Andorra	Andorrian Peseta	ADP
Angola	Kwanza	AOK
Argentina	Austral	ARA
Australia	Australian $	AUD
Austria	Schilling	ATS
Bahamas	Bahama $	BSD
Bahrain	Dinar	BHD
Bangladesh	Taka	BDT
Barbados	Barbados $	BBD
Belgium	Belgian Franc	
	(1) Commercial	BEC
	(2) Financial	BEL
Belize	Belize $	BZD
Bermuda	Bermudian $	BMD
Bolivia	Bolivian Peso	BOP
Botswana	Pula	BWP
Brazil	Cruzado	BRC
Brunei	Brunei $	BND
Bulgaria	Lev	BGL
Burma	Kyat	BUK
Burundi	Burundi Franc	BIF
Canada	Canadian $	CAD
Cape Verde	Cape Verdi Escudo	CVE
Cayman Islands	Cayman Isles $	KYD

Country	Currency	SWIFT code
Chile	Chilean Peso	CLP
China	Renminbi Yuan	CNY
Colombia	Colombian Peso	COP
Costa Rica	Colon	CRC
Cuba	Cuban Peso	CUP
Cyprus	Cyprus £	CYP
Czechoslovakia	Koruna	CSK
Denmark	Danish Kroner	DKK
Djibouti	Djibouti Franc	DJF
Dominican Republic	Dominican Peso	DOP
Ecuador	Sucre	ECS
Egypt	Egyptian £	EGP
El Salvador	Colon	SVC
Ethiopia	Birr	ETB
Falkland Islands	Falkland Islands £	FKP
Fiji	Fiji Dollar	FJD
Finland	Finnish Markka	FIM
France	French Franc	FRF
Gambia	Dalasi	GMD
Germany (West)	Deutsche Mark	DEM
Ghana	Cedi	GHC
Gibraltar	Gibraltar £	GIP
Greece	Drachma	GRD
Guatemala	Quetzal	GTQ
Guinea-Bissau	Peso	GWP
Guyana	Guyana $	GYD
Haiti	Gourde	HTG
Honduras	Lempira	HNL
Hong Kong	Hong Kong $	HKD
Hungary	Forint	HUF
Iceland	Icelandic Krona	ISK
India	Indian Rupee	INR
Indonesia	Rupiah	IDR
Iran	Iranian Rial	IRR
Ireland	Punt	IEP
Iraq	Iraqi Dinar	IQD
Israel	Shekel	ILS
Italy	Lira	ITL
Jamaica	Jamaician $	JMD
Japan	Yen	JPY
Jordan	Jordanian Dinar	JOD
Kampuchea	Riel	KHR

Country	Currency	SWIFT code
Kenya	Shilling	KES
Korea (North)	Won	KPW
Korea (South)	Won	KRW
Kuwait	Kuwaiti Dinar	KWD
Laos	Kip	LAK
Lebanon	Lebanese £	LBP
Liberia	Liberian $	LRD
Libya	Libyan Dinar	LYD
Luxembourg	Luxembourg Franc	LUF
Macao	Pataca	MOP
Malagasy	Malagasy Franc	MGF
Malawi	Kwacha	MWK
Malaysia	Malaysian Ringgit	MYR
Maldives	Rufiyaa	MVR
Malta	Maltese Lira	MTL
Mauritania	Ouguiya	MRO
Mauritius	Mauritius Rupee	MUR
Mexico	Mexican Peso	MXP
Mongolia	Tugrik	MNT
Morocco	Dirham	MAD
Mozambique	Metical	MZM
Nepal	Nepalese Rupee	NPR
Netherlands	Guilder	NLG
Netherlands Antilles	Antillian Guilder	ANG
New Zealand	New Zealand $	NZD
Nicaragua	Cordoba	NIC
Nigeria	Naira	NGN
Norway	Norwegian Krone	NOK
Oman	Omani Rial	OMR
Pakistan	Pakistan Rupee	PKR
Panama	Balbao	PAB
Papua New Guinea	Kina	PGK
Paraguay	Guarani	PYG
Peru	Inti	PEI
Philippines	Philippine Peso	PHP
Poland	Zloty	PLZ
Portugal	Escudo	PTE
Qatar	Qatari Rial	QAR
Romania	Leu	ROL
Rwanda	Rwanda Franc	RWF
St Helena	St Helena £	SHP
Sao Tome & Principe	Dobra	STD

Country	Currency	SWIFT code
Saudi Arabia	Saudi Riyal	SAR
Seychelles	Seychelles Rupee	SCR
Sierra Leone	Leone	SLL
Singapore	Singapore $	SGD
Soloman Islands	Soloman Islands $	SBD
Somali Republic	Somali shilling	SOS
South Africa	Rand	ZAR
Spain	Peseta	ESP
Sri Lanka	Sri Lanka Rupee	LKR
Sudan	Sudanese £	SDP
Surinam	Surinam Guilder	SRG
Swaziland	Lilangeni	SZL
Sweden	Swedish Krona	SEK
Switzerland	Swiss Franc	CHF
Syria	Syrian £	SYP
Taiwan	New Taiwan $	TWD
Tanzania	Tanzanian Shilling	TZS
Thailand	Baht	THB
Tonga	Palanga	TOP
Trinidad & Tobago	Trinidad & Tobago $	TTD
Tunisia	Tunisian Dinar	TND
Turkey	Turkish Lira	TRL
Uganda	Ugandian Shilling	UGS
United Kingdom	Pound Sterling	GBP
United States	US $	USD
Uruguay	Uruguayan Peso	UYP
United Arab Emirates	UAE Dirham	AED
USSR	Rouble	SUR
Vanuato	Vatu	VUV
Venezuela	Bolivar	VEB
Vietnam	Dong	VND
Western Samoa	Tala	WST
Yemen (North)	Rial	YER
Yemen (South)	Yemeni Dinar	YDD
Yugoslavia	New Yugoslavian Dinar	YUD
Zaire	Zaire	ZRZ
Zambia	Kwacha	ZMK
Zimbabwe	Zimbabwe $	ZWD

GLOSSARY

SUMMARY

This book is written on a subject normally dealt with in a treasury department. Treasurers have built up their own vocabulary of technical terms which it has been necessary to use for consciseness. As the reader may not be familiar with these terms, or their useage by treasurers, a glossary is provided.

Alphabetic glossary

Arbitrage—The exploitation of price differences to make a quick profit.

Bandbreite—The spread within which foreign exchange rates, in a regulated system, may move.

Barter—The exchange of goods rather than money. Can also be called countertrade.

Basis point—One ten thousandth of a unit of currency (*Note*. There is a different meaning when used in relation to interest rates).

Bid rate—The price at which a dealer will buy currency.

Blocked currency—A currency which is not freely convertible.

Break—a sudden fall in an FX rate.

Broken date—A future date which is not an exact multiple of FX periods into the future. It is not overnight, one week, two weeks, three weeks, one month etc. A period of three weeks and one day would end in a broken day.

Broker (FX)—An agent who brings together counter-parties wishing to buy and sell currency. The agent charges a commission for this service.

Business day—A day on which the FX market trades. It is important for any one deal that the FX markets for all the currencies involved are open on the value dates of the deal.

Cable—The sterling/US dollar FX rate.

CBOT—The Chicago Board of Trade, an important US futures and options exchange.

Closing rate—The exchange rate between currencies ruling at the end of the period in question.

121

Conglomerate—A commonly owned business group spanning a diverse range of products and businesses.

Contract date—The date on which an FX deal is agreed.

Contract rate—The agreed rate for an FX deal.

Conversion—The exchange of one currency for another.

Convertible currency—A currency freely exchangeable for any other (ie no governmental restriction on conversion).

Copey—The Danish kroner in dealer's slang.

Crawling, or adjustable, peg—Currency devaluation taking place at uncertain intervals in small steps, to discourage currency speculation. The rate is often based on the rise in the internal wholesale price level, less the estimated average inflation of the main trading partners of the country.

Currency basket—A selection of currencies used to value a specific item. The Special Drawing Right and the European Currency Unit are such items. A country may also link its currency to a basket of other currencies.

Current exchange rate—The present value of one currency in terms of other currencies.

Delivery date—The date on which funds are transferred.

Deposits or depo—funds deposited with a financial institution.

Discount or premium on a forward contract—The foreign currency amount of the contract forward rate and the spot rate at the date of inception of the contract (US Financial Accounting Standards Board Statement Number 52 definition).

ECGD—The Export Credit Guarantee Department of the UK Department of Trade, offers insurance for exports to UK exporters on basically commerical terms.

ECU—The European Currency Unit is a ten-element currency basket made up of currencies from the European Economic Community.

Effective interest rates—Interest rates adjusted for compounding distortions. Annualising is the normal method whereby a rate is shown which, compounded annually would yield the same amount of annual interest as the non annual interest rate input into the calculation. Only when interest rates for varying terms have been annualised (or given any common base period) can they be objectively compared.

Eurobank—A subsidiary of a major bank responsible for Euromarket dealing.

Euromarkets—The non domestic financial market based in Europe. Other areas tend to be described differently, such as the Singapore-based Asiadollar market. The Euromarket can be split into two aspects. The 'market' aspect (new currency creation and trading) and the 'nonmarket' aspect (fixed long-term currency holdings) (Machlup, 1970).

Exotic currencies—Currencies which do not have a large international market.

Exposure (FX)—Essentially the literal meaning. Subjecting an item to fluctuations in value as currency exchange rates move.

FASB—The US Financial Accounting Standards Board is the authority responsible for setting standards for published accounts in the USA. Standard Number 8 is now superseded by Number 52 and relates to the reporting of the effects of currency fluctuations. The Securities and Exchange Commission also sets standards for reports that are required to be made to that body; some of which are subsequently published.

Fisher effect—The theory (named after the eminent economist Irving Fisher) that movements in exchange rates balance differences in the interest rate ruling for those currencies.

Foreign exchange market—Dealings in FX organised mainly by banks and FX brokers.

Foreign exchange risk—The systematic risk associated with a foreign currency denominated return (or cost) stream and measured by the covariance between the rate of change of the exchange rate and the domestic market return (Wurster, 1978).

Forward Contract—An agreement to exchange, at a specified future date, currencies of different countries at a specified rate (the forward rate)

Functional currency—An entity's functional currency, is the currency of the primary economic environment in which the entity operates and primarily generates and expends cash. This concept is central to the application of US accounting standard FASB 52.

Futures (FX)—A type of forward contract which has been gaining popularity recently. A futures contract puts a present value on a financial transaction yet to take place. Currency futures are very similar to a bank forward contract but it is transacted on a futures exchange. There are also interest rate futures which put a value on future interest rates.

Hard currency—A currency which is generally considered to maintain a high value. Such currencies are normally low inflation currencies.

Hedge—A method of removing an exposure by producing a complementary exposure, partly or wholly to cancel out the first exposure.

IMM—The International Money Market, an important Chicago futures and options exchange.

Indication quote—This is an FX price supplied as an example of current prices. It is not an offer to deal at that price.

Ladder—A dealer's position report showing his forward deals by their maturity date, with the net position for each future date.

LIBID—The London interbank bid price.

LIMEAN—The mid-price between the London interbank bid and offer price.

LIBOR—The London interbank offer rate.

Limit move—The maximum permitted price move in one futures or option trading session. When the maximum is reached, trading is suspended whilst further margin calls are made.

Long positions—A net asset holding of a currency. If a company held more assets in sterling than it has sterling liabilities, it would be said that the company was 'long' of sterling.

Market-maker—A dealer in the FX market who is willing to consistently quote buying and selling prices when approached.

Margin calls—Demands for security to cover futures or option exchange trading. The demand is by the clearing house managing the futures or option exchange. Writers of options and buyers and sellers of futures have to deposit margin amounts set by the clearing house.

Nostro account—A foreign currency account used for settling FX deals. The account would normally be in the main financial centre for that currency.

Option forward contract—A forward contract which has a range of maturity dates. The purchaser of the forward can nominate which date to mature all, or some of the contract, at any time between the first and final maturity dates. All the contract has to be matured by the final maturity date.

Options—Contracts giving the purchaser the right, but not the obligation, to complete transactions at a pre-arranged price (the strike price) within a set period. 'American' options can be exercised at any time in the term of the option, whilst 'European' options can only be exercised at the maturity of the option. The writer of an option charges the buyer of an option, a premium normally when the option is first granted in consideration for the exercise rights granted.

Overshooting—A tendency by FX rates to continue a movement for longer than would seem justified by the circumstances.

Paris—The French franc in dealer's slang.

Realised differences—Arise from the sale or disposal of any kind of goods, services, assets or liabilities.

Reporting currency—The currency in which the ultimate holding enterprise presents its financial statements for shareholders.

Rollover—To replace a deal at maturity with one of similar value, as if the original deal were extended.

Settlement risk—The risk of the counter-party to an FX deal not completing his part of the contract cash payment.

Short position—A net liability holding of an enterprise. If the enterprise held more liabilities in sterling than it had sterling assets, then it would be 'short' of sterling.

Spot—For immediate effect. In domestic currency, spot would normally imply transacting the same day. Foreign currencies in the Euromarket have a clearing period of two days. Therefore spot foreign currency transactions take place two days after the dealing day. It is sometimes possible to obtain a one-day clearing in the Euromarket and this is referred to as 'tomorrow-next'.

Spread—The difference between the bid and offer price which represents a dealers profit margin.

Stocky—The Swedish krona in dealer's slang.

Stop loss—A conditional order to complete an FX deal when market rates reach a certain level.

Swaps—A term which has had various usages in the past, but currently refers to currency swaps or interest rate swaps. A currency swap has the same effect as a forward deal, but with an initial exchange of currencies which is reversed at the maturity date. It is usually used in conjunction with an interest rate swap rather than on its own. The usual form of interest rate swap, is an exchange of fixed interest rate funds for floating rate funds. No principal sums need pass between the parties as such sums are equal and opposite. All that passes is a net interest differential at the end of each prearranged period.

Swissy—The Swiss franc in dealer's slang.

Tom next—Short for tomorrow next day. It is a deal starting tomorrow and maturing on the next business day.

Transaction differences—In normal usage this is the same as realised differences. FASB 52 has an alternative definition of differences arising on conversion from the currency of denomination of the item to the functional currency of a business.

Treasurer—The corporate officer with the duty to obtain funds needed to conduct the business and to safeguard cash and other assets.

Unrealised exchange differences—Conversion differences on any item held by a business which is still retained at the end of the period in question.

BIBLIOGRAPHY

SUMMARY

Listed below are references from books, articles and television programmes. The bulk of them are mentioned in the text, but some first appear here as additional references if you require them. Where possible the reference is specific as to wherein the work the relevant part can be found. In many cases other parts of the quoted work merit study if you have the time.

Bibliography in alphabetic order

Abraham G M (1978) *Foreign Exchange Management and the Multinational Corporation* (Praeger Publishers, New York, 1978) p 203.

Abrams R K (1980) 'International Trade Flows Under Flexible Exchange Rates' Federal Reserve Bank of Kansas City Economic Review, March 1980 pp 3–10.

Abrams R K (1980) *Exchange Rate Volatility and Bilateral Trade Flows* (Federal Reserve Bank of Kansas City; unpublished).

Adair J (1985) *Management Decision Making* (Gower Publishing, London) (reviewed in Financial Decisions, April 1985, p 28).

Agmon T and Eldor R (1983) 'Currency Options Cope with Uncertainty' Euromoney, May 1983 p 227.

Allen D (1985) 'Small Within Big is Beautiful: Strategic Financial Management' Accountancy Age, 17 January 1985 p 31.

Antl B and Borsuk M (1980) *Eurocurrency Market; Currency Risk* (Euromoney Publications, London, 1980) p 61.

Arntz K (1984), Cashmap 'The (almost) Totally Computerised Treasurer' The Treasurer, Vol 6, No 10, November 1984 pp 47–49.

Artus J R (1978) 'Methods of Assessing the Long-Run Equilibrium Value of an Exchange Rate' Journal of International Economics 1978.

Ascher K and Kind J (1985) 'Industry Gets a Raw Deal from Financial Training' Financial Decisions, April 1985 pp 56–57.

Ashworth W (1975) *A Short History of the International Economy Since 1850* (3rd edn, Longman, London, 1975) p 302.

Babbel D F (1982) 'Exchange-rate Fluctuations and Transaction Exposure in the Multinational Corporation' I.E.E. PROC., Vol 129, Pt A, No 4, June 1982 pp 261–264.

Bailey P (1985) 'Company Finance Departments Take a New Look' Accountancy, Vol 96, No 1100, April 1985 p 71.

Bailey R (1985) 'What the Pound Could Gain from the EMS' The Accountant, Vol 192, No 5732, 7 March 1985 p 31.

Bannock G, Baxter R E and Rees R (1984) *Dictionary of Economics* (3rd edn, Penguin Books, London, 1984) p 161.

Barro R J (1984) *Macroeconomics* (John Wiley & Sons, New York, 1984) p 14.

Beresford P and Pearson K (1985) 'Dollar Sales Leave All Logic Behind' The Sunday Times, No 8379, 10 March 1985 p 65.

Bergsten F C and Cline W R (1982) *Trade Policy in the 1980's* (Institute for International Economics, Washington DC) 1982.

Bhandari J S (1981) 'Exchange Rate Overshooting Revisited' The Manchester School, Vol 49, No 2 pp 165–172.

Bilson J (1984) 'Why Be So Pessimistic' Euromoney, London, August 1984 p 154.

Bird J (1985) 'Big, Blue and Booming' The Sunday Times, No 8376, 17 February 1985 p 65.

Blackhurst R and Tumlir J (1978) 'Trade Relations Under Flexible Exchange Rates' GATT Studies in International Trade, No 8, 1978.

Blake V (1980) *Long Term Forward Contracts; Currency Risk* (Euromoney Publications, London, 1980) pp 94–95.

Blake V (1982) *Currency Swaps and Long Term Forwards; The Management of Foreign Exchange Risk* (Euromoney Publications, London, 1982) pp 196–200.

Blin J M, Greenbaum S I and Jacobs D P (1981) *Flexible Exchange Rates and International Business* (British North America Committee, 1981).

Blundell-Wignall A and Chouraqui J-C (1984) 'The Exchange Market Intervention' National Westminster Bank Quarterly Review, November 1984 p 60.

Boogaerde P V D (1984) 'The Private SDR' IMF Staff Papers; IMF, Washington DC, Vol 31, No 1, March 1984 pp 25–61.

Borsuck M (1982) *Yen Hedging and Investment Techniques; The Management of Foreign Exchange Risk* (Euromoney Publications, London, 1982) pp 210–214.

Briggs P W (1984) 'Foreign Exchange Offers Potential' Accountancy Age, 17 April 1984 p 20.

Brittain S (1984) 'The Future has not yet Happened' Financial Times, No 29212, 5 January 1984 p 17.

Brittain S (1985) 'The Serpent in the Dollar Paradise' Financial Times, No 29562, 28 February 1985 p 13.

Brooke M Z and Buckley P J (1982) *Handbook of International Trade* (Kluner, London, 1982) p 2.6.09.

Brooke M Z and Remmers H (1978) *The Strategy of Multinational Enterprise* (Pitman, London, 1978) p 68.

Brown B (1985) *Japanese Investment* (The Business Programme, UK Channel 4 Television, 17 February 1985).

Budd A (1985) *Exchange Instability* (The Business Programme UK Channel 4 Television, 20 January 1985).

Budd A (1987) *Group of Five Meeting* (The Business Programme, UK Channel 4 Television, 22 February 1987).

Buiter W H and Miller M (1981) 'Monetary Policy and International Competitiveness' Oxford Economic Papers, Vol 33 supplement, 1981 pp 143–175.

Butler S (1987) 'Why Aiwa Set Up in Singapore' Financial Times, No 30173, 2 March 1987 p 12.

Cane A (1983) 'Blue Tinged View of Worldwide Funds' Financial Times, No 29169, 11 November 1983 p 12.

Cane A (1987) 'ADP Leapfrogs into the World of Stock Quote Systems Financial Times, No 30162, 17 February 1987 p 12.

Carey M (1983) 'The Most International Accounting Standard' Accountancy, Vol 94, No 1078, July 1983 pp 13–15.

Carter H and Partington I (1981) *Applied Economics in Banking and Finance* (Oxford University Press, Oxford, 1981) p 289.

Channon D F and Jalland M (1979) *Multinational Strategic Planning* (Macmillan, London, 1979) p 143.

Child J (1984) *Organisation* (2nd edn, Harper and Row, London, 1984) p 146.

Clark P B (1973) 'Uncertainty, Exchange Risk and the Level of International Trade' Western Economic Journal, 1973.

Clark P B and Haulk C (1972) *Flexible Exchange Rates and the Level of Trade: A Preliminary Analysis of the Canadian Experience* (unpublished, Federal Reserve Board).

Clay M (1985) 'Exchange Rates: Cause of a Problem or Just an Excuse' Accountancy, Vol 96, No 1101, May 1985 p 123.

Clements A (1985) *ICI Abroad* (The Business Programme, UK Channel 4 Television, 20 January 1985).

Close R (1985) 'Survey of Current Practices, UK Exporters to Europe' Centre for Physical Distribution Management, Corby, UK, January 1985 p 4.

Cluff E (1985) 'Counting the Cost of System Maintenance' Computing, The Magazine, 18 April 1985 p 31.

Cockcroft J (1985) 'Coming Home' Banking World, Vol 3, No 1, January 1985 p 33.

Colchester N (1985) 'Wistful View of Exchange Rates' Financial Times, No 29520, 10 January 1985 p 13.

Cornell B and Dietrich J K (1978) 'The Efficiency of the Market for Foreign Exchange Under Floating Exchange Rates' Review of Economics and Statistics, February 1978 pp 111–120.

Cowe R (1985) 'Tackling Treasury with Computers' Financial Decisions, February 1985 p 55.

Crawford M (1985) 'Third World Debt is Here to Stay' Lloyds Bank Review, No 155, January 1985 p 13.

Crockett A (1979) *Money—Theory, Policy and Institutions* (2nd edn, Thomas Nelson and Son, London, 1979) p 155.

Cunningham G M (1978) *An Accounting Research Framework for Multinational Corporations* (UMI Research Press, New York, 1978).

Cushman D O (1983) 'The Effects of Real Exchange Rate Risk on International Trade' Journal of International Economics, 1983.

Dale R (1985) *Foreign Exchange* (The Business Programme, UK Channel 4 Television, 17 February 1985).

Daniels J D, Ogram E W and Radebaugh L H (1979) *International Business: Environments and Operations* (2nd edn, Addison-Wesley, Reading, Mass, 1979) pp 182–184.

Davies A (1985) 'The UK Balance of Payments' Banking World, London, January 1985 p 50.

Davis S M (1979) *Managing and Organising Multinational Corporations* (Pergamon Press, New York, 1979) p 369.

Dennis G and Nellis J (1984) 'The EMS and UK Membership' Lloyds Bank Review, No 154, October 1984 pp 13–31.

Develle M (1984) 'Money and Capital Markets' Conjoncture, Banque Paribas, Paris, Vol 12, No 9, October 1984 p 151.

Donaldson H (1983) 'A Computer on Every Dealer's Desk' Euromoney, May 1983 p 225.

Dooley M P and Shafer J R (1976) 'Analysis of Short Run Exchange Rate Behaviour March 1973 to September 1975' International Finance Discussion Papers, New York Federal Reserve System, New York 1976.

Dornbusch R (1976) 'Expectations and Exchange Rate Dynamics' Journal of Political Economy, Vol 84, No 6 pp 1161–1176.

Driskill R (1981) 'Exchange Rate Overshooting, the Trade Balance and Rational Expectations' Journal of International Economics, Vol 11, No 3 pp 361–377.

Dunn A and Knight M (1982) *Export Finance* (Euromoney, 1982) p 8.

Dufey G and Giddy I H (1978) 'International Financial Planning: The Use of Market Based Forecasts' California Management Review, Fall 1978 pp 69–81.

Dufey G and Mirus R (1982) *Accounting Standards and Exposure Management; The Management of Foreign Exchange Risk* (Euromoney Publications, London, 1982) pp 35–42.

Duerr M G (1977) *Protecting Corporate Assets under Floating Currencies* (Research Report of the Conference Board, 1977).

Earl M (1985) 'Managing Currency Risk in Stages' The Treasurer, Vol 7, No 3, March 1985 p 46.

Evans T G, Folks W R and Jilling M (1978) *The Impact of FASB8 on the Exchange Risk Management Practices of Multinationals* (Financial Accounting Standard Board, Stanford, 1978).

Fama E F (1979) 'Efficient Capital Markets: A Review of Theory and Empirical Work' Journal of Finance, December 1979 pp 1129–1139.

Fama E F and Miller M H (1972) *The Theory of Finance* (Dryden Press, Hinsdale, Illinois, 1972) p 336.

Fernie M (1985) 'World Capital Markets' The Treasurer, Vol 7, No 2, February 1985 p 17.

Fildes C (1985) 'Dangers in Defusing the Dollar' Daily Telegraph, No 40294, 7 January 1985 p 15.

Fitzgerald M D (1983) *Financial Futures* (Euromoney Publications, London, 1983) p 161.

Fitzgerald N (1985) 'BP's Finance Unit Boosts Treasury Role' Accountancy Age, 10 January 1985 p 10.

Fleet K (1985) 'Central Banks Flex Their Market Muscles' The Times, No 62043, 23 January 1985 p 20.

Fleming S (1987) 'Volker Opposes Currency Scheme' Financial Times, No 30165, 20 February 1987 p 1.

Flexel J (1985) 'Responses to Foreign Exchange Exposure' The Accountant, Vol 192, No 5738, 25 April 1985 p 24.

Friedman M (1953) 'The Case for Flexible Exchange Rates' in *Essays in Positive Economics* (Chicago University, Chicago, 1953).

Galbraith J K (1974) *Economics and the Public Purse* (Andre Deutsche, London, 1974) p 320.

Gallant P (1985) *Electronic Treasury Management* (Woodhead-Faulkner, Cambridge, UK, 1985).

Gazioglou S (1982) *Exchange Rate Overshooting: Clarification and Extensions; Programme of Research into Small Macromodels* (Research Paper No 4, Queen Mary College, London).

Gazioglou S (1984) *Exchange Rate Overshooting: Clarification and Extensions* (The Manchester School, September 1984) p 320.

Giddy I H and Dufey G (1975) 'The Random Behaviour of Flexible Exchange Rates: Implications for Forecasting' Journal of International Business Studies, Spring 1975 pp 1–32.

Gillett P (1985) 'Managing Foreign Exchange Exposure' Accountancy, Vol 96, No 1101, May 1985 p 67.

Mur C J (1981) *Trade Financing* (Euromoney Publications, London, 1981) p 15.

Gray R (1984) 'Currency Market Heats Up' Financial Decisions, November 1984 p 26–27.

Grubel H G (1977) *The International Monetary System* (3rd edn, Penguin Books, London, 1977) p 120.

Hanson D G (1982) *Service Banking* (2nd edn, Institute of Bankers, London 1982) p 394.

Harris A (1987) 'When Persuasion is Not Enough' Financial Times, No 30160, 14 February 1987 p 1.

Harrison T (1985) 'Corporate Borrowers Find Wide Scope on the European Market' The Accountant, Vol 192, No 5733, 21 March 1985 p 22.

Hawthorne J (1981) *Theory and Practice of Money* (Heinemann, London, 1981) p 174.

Helleiner G K (1981) *The Impact of the Exchange Rate System on the Developing Countries* (UN DP, New York, April 1981).

Henney G (1985) 'Foreign Exchange Risk, Identification and Reporting Systems' The Treasurer, Vol 7, No 2, February 1985 p 67.

Hesketh B C K (1976) *Methods of Forecasting Foreign Exchange Movements* (transcript of Oyez conference Management of Foreign Currency, Inn on the Park, London, 29 April 1976) p 6.

Heywood J (1984) 'Using Currency Options' The Treasurer, Vol 6, No 2, February 1984 pp 7–9.

Heywood J (1985) *Using Futures, Forwards and Options Markets* (Adam & Charles Black, London, 1985).

Hieronymi O (1983) *The Impact of Floating Exchange Rates in Relative Prices, Uncertainty and Economic Activity* (Battelle Institute, Geneva, Switzerland, 1983).

Hill G (1985) 'The Australian Capital Market' The Treasurer, Vol 7, No 2, February 1985 p 43.

Hodson D (1985) 'The Corporate Treasurer as a Central Figure' The Accountant, Vol 192, No 5732, 7 March 1985 p 15.

Hogan W P and Pearce I F (1984) *The Incredible Eurodollar* (3rd edn, Unwin, London, 1984) p 165.

Hogg S (1985) 'No Room for Sleight of Hand in PSBR' The Times, No 62065, 18 February 1985 p 10.

Hood W C (1983) *Exchange Rate Volatility & World Trade* (IMF, Washington DC, dated 6 December 1983, but unpublished).

Hooper P and Kohlhagen S W (1978) 'The Effect of Exchange Rate Uncertainty on the Prices and Volume of International Trade' Journal of International Economics, November 1978.

Hosenball M and Whymant R (1985) 'Trade War Across the Pacific' The Sunday Times, No 8379, 10 March 1985 p 67.

Humble J (1975) *The Responsible Multinational Enterprise* (The Foundation for Business Responsibility, London, 1975) p 23.

Irving J (1981) *The City at Work* (Andre Deutsch, London, 1981) p 127.

Jacquillat B and Solnik B (1978) *Multinational Firms Stock Price Behaviour* (North Holland Publishing Company, Amsterdam, 1978) p 232.

Acque L J (1981) 'Management of Foreign Exchange Risk' a Review Article, Journal of International Business Studies, Spring/Summer 1981 p 82.

Jay P (1985) 'There is No Button Labelled "Panic", nor is there One Called "Confidence"' Banking World, Vol 3, No 1, January 1985 p 28.

Jaycobs R (1984) 'Getting it Right at the Right Time' Euromoney, August 1984 p 154.

Johnson H G (1969) *The Case for Flexible Exchange Rates, 1969; UK and*

Floating Exchanges (International Economic Association, London, 1969) pp 9–37.

Jones G (1985) 'Currency and Interest Rate Swaps' The Treasurer, Vol 7, No 1, January 1985 pp 27–29.

Jones M and Lipsey D (1985) 'Thatcher Ready to Let Pound Equal Dollar' The Sunday Times, No 8371, 13 January 1985 p 1.

Kahnamouyipour H (1980) 'Forward Exchange' Accountancy, Vol 91, No 1046, October 1980 p 55.

Kaletsky A (1985) 'The Dollar and Foreign Investors' Financial Times, No 29544, 7 February 1985 p 15.

Kemp D S (1981) *Hedging Long-term Financings; The Essentials of Treasury Management* (Euromoney Publications, 1981) pp 115–121.

Kenen P B (1979) *Exchange Rate Variability: Measurement and Implications* (International Finance Section, Princeton University, 30 June 1979).

Kern D (1982) *Fundamental Analysis; The Management of Foreign Exchange Risk* (Euromoney Publications, 1982) p 56.

Kettell B (1979) *The Finance of International Business* (Graham and Trotman; London, 1979) p 67.

Kettell B (1984) 'How to Cope with New Currency Translation Rules' International Finance and Accountancy Report, Vol 1, No 5, May 1984 p 5.

Keynes J M (1936) *The General Theory of Employment, Interest and Money* (Macmillan, London, 1936) p 383.

Kohlhagen S W (1975) 'The Performance of the Foreign Exchange Markets 1971–74' Journal of International Business Studies, Fall 1975 pp 33–39.

Kolde E J (1974) *The Multinational Company* (D C Heath & Co, New York, 1974) p 67.

Kreinen M E and Heller H R (1974) 'Adjustment Costs, Optimal Currency Areas and International Reserves' ch 6 of *International Trade and Finance—Essays in Honour of Jan Tinbergen* (International Arts and Sciences Press, 1974).

Lalls S (1980) *The Multinational Corporation* (Macmillan, London, 1980) p 114.

Lamfalussy A (1983) *Foreign Exchange Risk- 1985* (Financial Times Conference, London, February 1983).

Lanyi A and E Suss (1982) 'Exchange Rate Variability: Alternative Measures and Interpretation' *Staff Papers* (IMF, Washington DC. December 1982).

Lee Pemberton R (1984) 'The Role and Future of the International Institutions' Bank of England Quarterly Bulletin, Vol 24, No 4, December 1984 pp 503–510.

Levich R M (1980) *Use and Evaluation of Foreign Exchange Forecasts; Currency Risk* (Euromoney Publications, London, 1980) p 98.

Levich R M (1982) *Composite Forecasts; The Management of Foreign Exchange Risks* (Euromoney Publications, London, 1982) pp 98–101.

Lipsey D (1985) 'New Weapon Needed to Fight the Dollar' The Sunday Times, No 8379, 10 March 1985 p 65.

Lipsey D and Beresford P (1985) 'Britain Goes Dollar-wise' The Sunday Times, No 8378, 3 March 1985 p 65.

Logue D E and Sweeny R J (1977) 'White Noise in Imperfect Markets: The Case for the Franc-Dollar Exchange Rate' The Journal of Finance, June 1977 pp 761–768.

Loehnis A (1984) *Fluctuating Exchange Rates* (British Institute of Management, 2nd Annual International Conference, London, October 1984).

Lyden B and Underwood T (1983) 'Computer Systems for the Corporate Treasurer' The Treasurer, Vol 5, No 9, October 1983 p 22.

McCulloch R (1983) 'Unexpected Real Consequences of Floating Exchange Rates' *Essays in International Finance* (No 153, Princeton University, 1983).

Machlup F (1970) 'Euro-Dollar Creation: A Mystery Story' Banca Nazionale Del Lavoro Quarterly Review, September 1970 p 221.

McKenney J L and Keen P G W (1980) *Readings in Managerial Psychology* (3rd edn, University of Chicago Press, Chicago, Ill, 1980) p 138.

McKinnon R I (1978) *Exchange Rate Instability, Trade Balances and Monetary Policy in Japan and the United States* (IMF, Washington DC, 1978).

Macrae N (1985) *The 2024 Report* (Sidgwick and Jackson, London).

Merrick S (1985) *Micro-Treasurer, a Treasury Management System* (Swallow Business Systems, London, 1985) pp 1–4.

Mishan E J (1982) *Cost-Benefit Analysis* (3rd edn, George Allen and Unwin, London, 1982) p 364.

Moreland R J (1985) 'Decline of Sterling' The Times, No 62036, 15 January 1985 p 2.

Morita A (1983) *A New International Currency System* (Joint Keidanren/Group of Thirty Forum, Tokyo, April 1983).

Morrison D (1982) *Interest Rates; The Management of Foreign Exchange Risk* (Euromoney Publications, London, 1982) pp 81–87.

Murfin A and Ormerod P (1983) *The Forward Rate for the US Dollar and the Efficient Markets Hypothesis 1978–1983* (The Henley Centre for Forecasting, November 1983).

Nevin E T (1981) *Text Book of Economic Analysis* (5th edn, Macmillan, London, 1981) p 512.

Newbold G D, Buckley P J and Thurwell J C (1978) *Going International* (Associated Business Press, London, 1978) p 140.

Newman P (1985) 'London Boom in Currency "Bets"' Daily Mail, London, 10 March 1985 p 25.

Niehaus J (1977) 'Exchange Rate Dynamics with Stock/Flow Interreactions' Journal of Political Economy, Vol 85, No 6 pp 1245–1257.

Officer L H (1976) *The Purchasing Power Parity Theory of Exchange Rates* (IMF Staff Papers, Washington D C, March 1976).

Ogley B (1981) *Business Finance* (Longman, London, 1981) pp 436–437.

O'Neill J (1984) 'The ECU as a Financial Instrument for Risk Diversification' The Business Economist, Vol 15, No 2, Summer 1984 p 35.

Pearson K (1985) 'Dollar Hits IBM's Calculations' The Sunday Times, No 8371, 13 January 1985 p 2.

Perlmutter H V (1968) 'Super-Giant Firms in the Future' Wharton Quarterly, Penn, USA, Winter 1968.

Perlmutter H V (1973) *Top Management* (Longman, London, 1973) pp 329–343.

Perry F E (1981) *The Elements of Banking* (3rd edn, Methuen, London) p 69.

Perry F E (1983) *A Dictionary of Banking* (2nd edn, Macdonald & Evans, Plymouth, UK, 1983) p 25.

Pigott C, Sweeny R and Willett T D (1975) *Some Aspects of the Behaviour and Effects of Exchange Rate Flexibility* (Konstanz Conference, Switzerland, June 1975).

Plasschaert S R F (1979) *Transfer Pricing and Multinational Corporations* (European Centre for Study and Information on Multinational Corporations, Saxon House, Farnborough, Hants, UK, 1979) p 60.

Plender J (1987) 'Capital Flows and Gunboats' Financial Times, No 30173, 2 March 1987 p 10.

Poole W (1967) 'Speculative Prices as Random Walk. An Analysis of Ten Time Series of Flexible Exchange Rates' Southern Economic Journal, April 1967 pp 468–478.

Porter M M (1971) *A Theoretical and Empirical Framework for Analysing the Term Structure of Exchange Rate Expectations* (IMF Staff Papers, IMF, Washington DC, November 1971) pp 613–645.

Prasad B (1976) *An Introduction to Multinational Management* (Prentice-Hall, Englewood Cliff, NJ, USA, 1976) p 49.

Quinn E (1984) 'CAP Aims at Money Dealers' Computing the Newspaper, 29 November 1984 p 33.

Quinn E (1985) 'Reuters Aims to Protect its Lead in Dealing Rooms' Computing the Newspaper, 7 March 1985 p 25.

Raemy-Dicks C (1981) *Trade Financing* (Euromoney Publications, London, 1981) p 17–19.

Ramond C (1984) 'Trends are Fine for Some Currencies' Euromoney, August 1984 p 157.

Reier S (1984) 'Insurers Just Getting the Hang of FX Risk' Institutional Investor, London November 1984 p 265.

Reiss J (1980) 'Currency Risk' Accountancy, Vol 191, No 1039, March 1980 p 106.

Richardson G (1983) 'British Economic Policy over the Last Decade' Bank of England Quarterly Bulletin, June 1983.

Ricks D A (1978) *International Dimensions of Corporate Finance* (Prentice-Hall, Englewood Cliffs, NJ USA, 1978) p 32.

Robinson W (1983) *After 10 Years of Floating Exchange Rates, Does Purchasing Parity Theory Have Any Relevance?* (Management of Foreign Exchange Risk, Conference, London, 14–15 November 1983).

Rodriguez R M (1976) *International Financial Management* (Prentice-Hall, Englewood Cliffs, NJ, USA, 1976) p 96.

Rogalski R J and Vinso J D (1977) 'Price Level Variations as Predictors of Flexible Exchange Rates' Journal of International Business Studies, Spring/Summer 1977 pp 71–82.

Roll R W and Solnik B H (1975) *A Pure Foreign Exchange Asset Pricing Model* (European Institute for Advanced Studies in Management, Working Paper No 75, August 1975).

Rosenburg M R (1982) *Technical Analysis; The Management of Foreign Exchange Risk* (Euromoney Publications, London, 1982) pp 76–80.

Ross-Jackson J T (1983) 'A Model of Selective Cover of Currency Risk' Accountancy, April 1983, Vol 94, No 4 pp 108–111.

Ruck A (1981) *Using the Market; The Essentials of Treasury Management* (Euromoney Publications, London, 1981) pp 109–116.

Rudofsky J (1985) 'Exchange Set to Upstage LIFFE' Daily Telegraph, London, No 40392, 2 May 1985 p 12.

Rutterford J (1985) 'Convertibles: the Hybrid Security with Popular Appeal' The Accountant, Vol 192, No 5736, 11 April 1985 p 22–24.

Samuels J M and Wilkes F M (1980) *Management of Company Finance* (3rd edn, Nelson, London, 1980) p 481.

Shaw E R (1981) *The London Money Market* (3rd edn, Heinemann, London, 1981) p 127.

Shearlock P. (1985) 'Reducing Exposure to the Dollar' The Sunday Times, London, No 8380, 17 March 1985 p 21.

Shultz G P (1983) 'Statement to the US Senate Foreign Relations Committee' 15 February 1983.

Sieghart M A (1985) 'London Options this Month' Financial Times, London, No 29614, 2 May 1985 p 5.

Singer A (1984) 'Electronic Cash Sophistication' Certified Accountant, London, October 1984 p 24.

Smith D (1985) 'Volatile Dollar Poses Long Term Threat to Britain's Exporters' The Times, London, No 62075, 1 March 1985 p 25.

Spencer E W (1984) 'Co-operation with the Competition; Speaking of Japan' Keizai Koho Center, Tokyo, Vol 5, No 44, August 1984 p 7.

Spronck L H (1980) *The Financial Executive's Handbook for Managing Multinational Corporations* (John Wiley and Sons, New York, 1980) p 90.

Srodes J (1984) 'Weaker Dollar' Daily Telegraph, No 40289, 31 December 1984 p 21.

Stoner G (1985) 'Forward Dealing' Accountancy, Vol 96, No 1100, April 1985 p 72.

Taylor M (1985) 'Forward Exchange: De-mystifying the Dealing Room' The Accountant, Vol 192, No 5739, 2 May 1985 p 14.

Thursby M C (1981) 'The Resource Reallocation Costs of Fixed and Flexible Exchange Rates' Journal of Economics, November 1981.

Tsurumi Y (1977) *Multinational Management* (Ballinger, Cambridge, Mass, 1977) p 118.

Tudge D (1984) 'The SDR—A Neglected Alternative' The Treasurer, Vol 6, No 5, May 1984 p 37.

Tutt N (1985) 'Options Open on the Shape of Things to Come' Accountancy Age, 9 May 1985 p 8.

Tygier C (1982) *A Trader's Approach; The Management of Foreign Currency Risk* (Euromoney Publications, London) pp 117–120.

Tygier C (1983) *Basic Handbook of Foreign Exchange* (Euromoney Publications, London, 1983) p 32.

Urry M (1984) 'Swiss Franc; Switzerland-Banking and Finance' Financial Times, No 29505, 20 December 1984 p 7.

Vernon R and Wells L T (1976) *The Manger in the International Economy* (3rd edn, Prentice-Hall, Englewood Cliffs, NJ, USA, 1976) p 169.

Weisweiller R (1983) Foreign Exchange; Woodhead-Faulkner (Cambridge, UK, 1983) p 21.

Westerfield J M (1977) *The Causes and Effects of Exchange Rate Volatility; The International Monetary System: A Time of Turbulence* (AEI, USA, 1982).

Weston J F and Sorge B W (1977) *Guide to International Financial Management* (McGraw-Hill, New York, 1977) p 97.

Whittam Smith A (1984) 'Bank Prescribes Lower Interest Rates Medicine' Daily Telegraph, No 40283, 21 December 1984 p 15.

Wicks J (1984) 'The Economy; Switzerland-Banking and Finance' Financial Times, No 290505, 20 December 1984 p 7.

Williamson J (1983) *The Exchange System* (Institute of International Economics, USA, 1983).

Wilmot J, Hawkins J and Parry G (1984) *The International Treasury Report* (Bank of America, London, May 1984) p 34.

Wurster T S (1978) *The Firm in the International Economy* (Phd Dissertation, Yale University, 1978) p 25.

Wyss D (1982) *Econometrics; The Management of Foreign Exchange Risk* (Euromoney Publications, London, 1982) pp 62–75.

Yeager L B (1976) *International Monetary Relations* (Theory, History and Policy Group, New York, 1976).

Zenoff D B (1984) 'Looking Ahead for Treasury Management' The Treasurer, Vol 6, No 11, December 1984 pp 27–38.

INDEX